G. H H. Del. T. Picken, Lith. George Routledge & Co. London & New York. Day & Son, Lithrs. to the Queen

OUTRAM & HAVELOCK'S PERSIAN CAMPAIGN

BY

CAPT. G. H. HUNT

78TH HIGHLANDERS

TO WHICH IS PREFIXED

A Summary of Persian History

AN ACCOUNT OF VARIOUS DIFFERENCES BETWEEN ENGLAND AND PERSIA, AND AN INQUIRY INTO THE ORIGIN OF THE LATE WAR

BY GEORGE TOWNSEND

The Naval & Military Press Ltd

Published by
The Naval & Military Press Ltd

PREFACE.

Captain Hunt's narrative requires no eulogium from my pen. It is a plain and graphic account of transactions in which that gallant officer took part. The Persian campaign is rendered celebrated from the fact that Generals Outram and Havelock, whose more recent deeds in India are now the theme of every tongue, were prominent actors in its stirring scenes. While these sheets were passing through the press, intelligence of Captain Hunt's sudden decease from an attack of cholera reached England. In him the country loses one of its best defenders; and the fact of his early death in a distant land, invests this record of the Persian campaign with peculiar interest. His memory will long be cherished with affectionate regret by his comrades, and his name, inscribed on the roll of British heroes, will be a household word amongst us.

Of Persia little is known in this country.

I have endeavoured to draw up from the works of the most trustworthy authorities, a summary of its history in both ancient and modern times. To this is added an account of various differences between England and Persia, and an inquiry into the origin of the late war. With respect to the latter, my object has been to furnish the reader with an accurate relation of facts, and I have therefore abstained from expressing opinions. That the Government embarked rashly in the conflict, without the sanction of Parliament—and that they accepted, after what was termed a successful campaign, conditions of peace less favourable than those offered at Constantinople previous to the outbreak of hostilities—cannot be denied. These matters have, however, been fully discussed in the columns of the different newspapers of the day; and in these pages will be found a simple record of the facts as they are set forth in the papers laid before the British Parliament.

G. T.

LONDON,
November, 1857.

CONTENTS.

CHAPTER VII.

CHAPTER VIII.

CHAPTER IX.

CHAPTER X.

PERSIA.

CHAPTER I.

A short Account of the ancient Kingdom of Persia, and its Position amongst the early Principalities and Powers of the Earth.

MOST people accustomed to pay the slightest attention to current events are aware that Great Britain has been recently involved in a contest with Persia, though few make any efforts to acquire knowledge respecting the early career of this remarkable state, the various vicissitudes and transformations it has undergone, or the splendours of its past history.

Accurate and concise information upon these points will, it is imagined, form an appropriate introduction to its modern history, a narrative of the late war, and the record of the daring achievements of British warriors. With this object in view, the editor of the present volume has endeavoured to give, within as small a compass as possible, a sketch of the previous career of this celebrated state.

Most of the nations that now play a prominent part in the world are entirely of modern creation. They arose amid the new order of things that grew out of the disruption of the old Roman dominion, and are, therefore, essentially modern in their character, development, and government. This is not, however, the case with Persia. It is one of the most ancient powers of the world, which, after innumerable vicissitudes and changes, continues to occupy a prominent position in the later system. A dispassionate review of its previous history will, therefore, enable us to form some definite conclusions as to its actual importance, and to arrive at a just idea of the consideration to which it is entitled. Such a review naturally falls under the two great classifications, ancient and modern, and to the former of these inquiries we propose to direct attention, in this preliminary chapter.

The tenacity of national life displayed by

Persia is truly remarkable. The continued existence of this state may be regarded as a great fact: it is a material guarantee for the authenticity of many historical records, sacred and profane. The prominent events in the early experience of this kingdom, and the high destinies to which it was called in the youth of the world, fortunately do not rest solely upon the testimony of Persian chroniclers; for her writers, from time immemorial, have enjoyed an unenviable notoriety for the recklessness with which they mingled fiction with truth. Whenever what they imagined to be the glory of their country rendered it necessary for them to create a dynasty, or to record a series of brilliant achievements, these falsifiers of history boldly filled in the canvas, and told of events that had never happened, or conjured up a long array of warriors, philanthropists, and statesmen, who existed only in their glowing imaginations. After this method, sanguinary triumphs which never stained the earth with slaughter were recounted, and many impossible achievements narrated.

Whilst Warton was building up his theory,

that romantic fiction originated during the Crusades, and was disseminated by the Arab conquerors of Europe, he did not attribute sufficient importance to the fact that, at a date long anterior to that which he assigned for its rise, the Persian writers had created the whole machinery of romance. Their fabulous ages stretched backward to a period far beyond the date usually fixed upon for the creation of man, and the delightful era that has since charmed the minds of so many poets and philosophers, is shadowed forth in their early mythology. Peris and Dives, the good and evil spirits, gods, giants, and other creations of romance, figure prominently in many of their legends. Winged monsters, griffins, dragons, abound in the same marvellous stories; and a Persian hero triumphed over a monster of this kind, exactly as St. George, our patron saint, is said to have vanquished the dragon in our own popular legend.

To these sources may be traced the machinery that forms the basis of Gothic romance. Even Comus with his giddy rout, in Milton's "Masque," and Prospero and his attendant spirits, in Shakespeare's charming comedy of the "Tempest," are but a fuller development of the germs contained in the more brilliant specimens of the inventive powers of the Oriental mind. It is true that by the divine art of the poet these glowing creations of Asiatic poetry have been clothed in new forms, invested with fairer attributes, and adapted in spirit to our European civilization; but, for all that, the idea originated with those early poets and dreamers who trimmed the lamp of knowledge in remote and (in a certain sense) benighted ages. They were the true pioneers of our modern system of progression and improvement, and, when Asia was the seat of empire, and this world of ours was in its youth, acted the part of the instructors and entertainers of mankind.

The vulgar in our own day talk of *hocus-pocus* tricks, and few of their listeners would imagine that they were making use of an expression employed in that identical sense centuries before our era, and that "Hokopaz," in the ancient Persic tongue, signified a conjuror. In fact, the later researches of learned men fully bear out the opinion expressed by Hales, who says, "Persia, indeed, or Iran, from the earliest times, seems to have been the great classic ground of Oriental mythology and romance, which diverged and spread from thence with its roving tribes, the Palli and Pelasgi, &c., to almost every surrounding and distant country, both of the east and of the west. The fabled wars of the gods and giants, which pervade the Greek and Latin classics, most probably originated from the wars of their heroes, or ancient kings, with the Dives, or rebellious demons, in which they were supposed to be assisted by the Peris, or fairies, the good demons and guardian angels of mankind; both acting under the control of the Supreme Being."

The fact of the high antiquity of Persia does not, however, depend upon the testimony of profane writers, whether belonging to Persia, or other ancient or modern states; but is substantiated by several passages in the Bible. The sacred annals contain abundant evidences of the important position occupied by this state, when the Jews were a favoured people, and the Divine Governor of the Universe maintained a direct communication with a portion of the human race.

Persia, therefore, it must be admitted, is one of the most ancient governments upon the face of the globe. Although its territories have undergone many changes, and its rulers have fallen from the high estate which they once possessed, the present inhabitants of Persia dwell upon the same tracts of land that were occupied by their remote ancestors in the early ages of the world. In this respect they enjoy a great advantage over their rivals in antiquity—the Jews and the Arabs—who have no abiding city. The Jews are scattered over the face of the earth, preserving their distinctive marks of separation, without possessing a country which they can call their own, while the Arabs have from time immemorial been wanderers in the desert. The Persians alone, of all the nations who were their early contemporaries, have preserved their nationality, and retained possession of, at least, a portion of those territories in which they dwelt when Daniel wrote his prophecies, and the

Jews were about to forfeit their high prerogatives.

The Persian chroniclers, from remote ages, recorded the acts of their kings, and the chief events of the time. Whatever their monarchs said or did was carefully noted down, and they were continually attended by scribes or secretaries, whose duty it was to register their words and actions. In all festivals and public ceremonies these functionaries might be seen performing their duties; and even amid the tumult of battle they zealously pursued their occupation. The institution prevailed amongst the Asiatic nations, and many notices of the same are found in Scripture. It may seem strange to the modern student that all these records should have perished, with the exception of some edicts preserved in the Scripture narratives of Ezra and Nehemiah. Notices of the Persian sovereigns and their subjects also occur in the writings of some of the later prophets, and the Book of Esther contains a picture of the manners of the Persian court, with an account of its splendours and magnificence.

The Jews and the Persians, at the period of which it treats, lived in friendly intercourse; and the Jewish maiden, Esther, was raised from her low estate to share the Persian monarch's throne. This was supposed to be Ahasuerus, who reigned over one hundred and twenty-seven provinces, and his greatness and power are thus summed up in the last chapter of the Book of Esther:—"And the king Ahasuerus laid a tribute upon the land and upon the isles of the sea. And all the acts of his power and of his might, and the declaration of the greatness of Mordecai, whereunto the king advanced him, are they not written in the book of the chronicles of the kings of Media and Persia? For Mordecai the Jew was next unto king Ahasuerus, and great among the Jews, and accepted of the multitude of his brethren, seeking the wealth of his people, and speaking peace to all his seed."

According to the Persian historians, their empire was founded about three thousand years after the creation of the world. This, however, is one of those much-disputed questions of national origin that it will not be necessary for us to investigate in order to prove its fallacy. Upon the point of origin a nation's historians are generally permitted to indulge in speculations, since it would be difficult, if not altogether impossible, to trace with any degree of certainty the small tribes or congregations of families from which mighty nations and peoples invariably take their rise. We will, therefore, descend from the region of romance to the common-place arena in which we may hope to meet with narrations more entitled to be regarded as matter of fact. The extent of Persia, at the earliest periods of which we possess certain knowledge, was small in comparison to that which it subsequently attained. Like Napoleon at the zenith of his fame, the Persian autocrats wielded the sceptre of authority over many neighbouring states, and the descendants of those who had been little more than patriarchal chieftains, possessed for a time the empire of the world.

The ancient state which we call Persia was contained within the tract of country bounded on the west by the river Euphrates and

Media, on the south by the Persian Gulf and the Indian Ocean, on the north by the Great Desert and the Caspian Sea, and on the east by the rivers Indus and Oxus. Its limits, consequently, underwent various alterations, as the wave of conquest rolled back its warriors or bore them proudly forward in triumph upon its crest. The people were, at the commencement, a race of shepherds and mountaineers, subdivided into several hordes or tribes. Herodotus (ix. 122) tells us:—"The Persians originally occupied a small and rugged country;" and Plato, who lived in the flourishing times of the Persian monarchy, confirms this in a remarkable manner (The Laws, iii. c. 12). "The Persians were originally a nation of shepherds and herdsmen, occupying a rude country, such as naturally fosters a hardy race of people, capable of supporting both cold and watching, and, when needful, of enduring the toils of war." They were known as Persæ, and the province in which they dwelt was called Persis; and thus, as was often the case, the name of the province and its populace has been retained for the large state which they afterwards founded. Its names were Paras, Fars, and in Scripture, Elam. Iran is, however, the term by which, both in ancient and modern times, the Persians have designated their country. Like all nomad tribes, they gradually extended the sphere of their depredations until their acquisitions enabled them to found a separate state, which assumed the dignity and consistency of a settled form of government. Herodotus tells us (i. 134), that the Medes, like the Persians, looked upon themselves as the first people in the world, and valued other nations in proportion as they were situated near them; esteeming those the least who are the most remote.

In the early Persian legends, the original seat of their race is described as a delicious country, named *Eriene-Veedjo.* Like most nations the Persians possessed numerous traditions, with reference to which the learned Heeren writes:—"The traditions of this race preserve some very important particulars respecting their descent, their ancient abodes, and their gradual dissemination through the land of Iran. These traditions are preserved in the beginning of the Vendidat, the most important, and, it is probable, the most ancient of all their sacred books, the collection of which is called the Zendavesta. The first two chapters of this work, entitled Fargards, contain the above traditions, not wrapped up in allegory, but so evidently historical as to demand nothing more than the application of geographical knowledge to explain them. With the exception of the Mosaical Scriptures, we are acquainted with nothing (the untranslated Vedas perhaps excepted) which so plainly wears the stamp of remote antiquity, ascending beyond the times within which the known empires of the East flourished; in which we catch, as it were, the last faint echo of the history of a former world, anterior to that great catastrophe of our planet which is attested in the vicinity of the parent country of these legends, by the remains of the elephant, the rhinoceros, and the mammoth, and other animals properly belonging to the countries of the South. It would be a fruitless labour to attempt to assign dates to these remains, but if the compiler of the Vendidat himself, who was long anterior to the Persian, and, as we shall have occasion to show, probably also to the Median dynasty, as known to us, received them as the primeval traditions of his race, our opinion of their importance may be fully justified." The high antiquity of the Persian language has also been pointed out by Sir William Jones, who believed it to have been the original Syriac or Chaldean, the parent of the Sanscrit, the Zend, and the Parsi, and to have furnished an important element in the Greek, Latin, and Gothic tongues.

Such were the people who in the earliest times of which we possess authentic records attracted the attention of their neighbours, and prepared to play an important part upon the stage of human life. Two dynasties, with a long interregnum between them, are supposed to have reigned in Persia previous to its conquest by Alexander of Macedon, B.C. 331. The former that of the Pischdadians, which lasted between five and six centuries, and the latter that of the Kaianites, which exceeded seven. The first ruler is said to have been

Kaiumarath, Keiomarras, or Kaiomurs, who was raised to the imperial dignity, B.C. 2190, according to Hales, and B.C. 890, according to Sir William Jones. The former date may be correct, as it does not seem improbable that soon after the dissolution of the first Assyrian empire, the Persian tribes should gradually rise into importance. By some authorities this monarch is declared to have been a grandson of Noah. The truth may be, that he was a descendant of Shem. He was succeeded by Hushang, surnamed Pischdad "the Just," or as Sir William Jones suggests, "the Legislator."

This prince was a favourite character in the old Persian romances. Certain writers have endeavoured to establish his identity with Chedorlaomer, king of Elam, one of the four monarchs who, in the fourteenth chapter of Genesis, are represented as making war upon five other kings. The latter were defeated and the victors carried off Lot, Abraham's brother, into captivity. The misfortunes of his relative aroused the ire of the patriarch, who armed his trained servants, pursued the aggressors, rescued Lot and the booty, and slew Chedorlaomer. The theory is ingenious, and has enabled Hales to assign certain occurrences in the early history of Persia to particular periods. By carrying it out, he has found another member of the Persian royal family, whose career, in some points, furnishes a counterpart to that of Nebuchadnezzar. These are, however, at the best, conjectures; and so little accurate information can be obtained of the early Persian rulers, or even of the limits of their reigns or the epochs in which they flourished, that we turn at once to fairer fields of investigation, in which the results are more definite, and the conclusions accordingly more satisfactory.

The most powerful of its ancient monarchs and the real founder of the great Persian empire, was Cyrus; and in treating of his life, we once more enter the domains of what may fairly be deemed authentic history. Previous to his accession, the Persians had led a nomad kind of life, and were, in a great measure, subject to the Medes; but he gave them permanent political institutions, and upon him the crowns of Babylon, Media, and Persia devolved,—the two latter by regular succession, and the former by right of conquest. Cyrus became a great conqueror, and the absolute dominion of Asia fell into his grasp. His mighty empire gradually swallowed up the surrounding states; and the reader may form a correct idea of its extent from the fact that it was bounded on the north by the Caspian and Euxine seas, on the south by Ethiopia and the sea of Arabia, on the east by the river Indus, and on the west by the Ægean. This great monarch, probably through the influence of Daniel, lived in close alliance with the Jews, and at one time issued a proclamation in their favour. The account given in the Scriptures of this remarkable transaction is as follows: —"Now, in the first year of Cyrus, king of Persia, that the word of the Lord spoken by the mouth of Jeremiah might be accomplished, the Lord stirred up the spirit of Cyrus, king of Persia, that he made a proclamation throughout all his kingdom, and put it also in writing, saying, Thus saith Cyrus, king of Persia, All the kingdoms of the earth hath the Lord

God of Heaven given me; and He hath charged me to build Him an house in Jerusalem, which is in Judah. Who is there among you of all His people? The Lord his God be with him, and let him go up."—(2 Chron. xxxvi. 22, 23.)

The decree was executed, but the great design of the restoration of the city and temple of the Jews remained unfinished at the death of Cyrus. His successor was his son Cambyses, a warlike prince, who delighted in conquest. He made war upon Egypt and Ethiopia, and perished from a wound which he accidentally inflicted upon himself as he was mounting his horse to set out upon his return to Persia. Cambyses treated the Jews with rigour, and in this conduct was imitated by his successor, Artaxerxes. (Circ. B.C. 520.)

Prideaux sums up the accounts derived from the sacred writings relative to this monarch's interference, in these terms:—"As soon as Artaxerxes was settled in the kingdom, after the death of Cambyses, the Samaritans wrote a letter to him, setting forth that the Jews were rebuilding their city and temple at Jerusalem; that, they having been always a rebellious people, there was reason to suspect that, as soon as they should have finished that work, they would withdraw their obedience from the king, and pay no more toll nor tribute, which might give an occasion for all Syria and Palestine to revolt also, and the king be excluded from having any more portion on that side the river Euphrates. And for the truth of what they had informed him of, as to the rebellious temper of that people, they referred him to the records of his predecessors, wherein they desired search might be made concerning this matter. On the receipt of this letter, examination being made, according to the purport of it, into the records of former times, concerning the behaviour of the Jews under the Assyrian and Babylonish empires, and it being found in them with what valour they had long defended themselves, and with what difficulty they were at length reduced by Nebuchadnezzar, an order was issued forth to prohibit them from proceeding any farther, and sent to the Samaritans to see it put in execution, who, immediately on the receipt thereof, went up to Jerusalem, and having exhibited their order to the Jews, made them desist, by force and power, from going on any farther with the work of the house; so it wholly ceased till the second year of Darius, king of Persia, for about the space of two years."

Upon the death of this prince, the usurpation of the Magians was resented, a fearful massacre of their order ensued, and a nobleman, named Ochus, was raised to the vacant throne, under the title of Darius I. This sovereign showed the Jews great favour, and under his auspices the restoration of their city and the erection of their temple were resumed. In order to improve the internal administration of the country, Darius divided it into satrapies. In fact, he accomplished more for the consolidation of the Persian empire than any of his predecessors had done. He first established the royal residence in certain fixed situations, in order to check the wandering habits of his subjects. The division of the empire into satrapies secured its better organization, and laid the foundations of that colossal system of dominion of which the disciplined hosts afterwards came into collision with the warrior levies of Greece and Rome.

Conquest appeared to be his passion, and Darius, or Hystaspes, attempted that of Greece, then gradually rising in importance. With this object, he assembled one of those mighty armaments which, in earlier ages, so often issued forth from Asia, spreading terror and desolation amongst the infant states of Europe. Darius sent ambassadors to demand submission in the usual form, by claiming the homage of earth and water; whereupon "the Athenians," Herodotus tells us, "threw his heralds into their pit of punishment, and the Lacedæmonians pitched them into wells, telling them to procure the earth and water there, and carry it to the king." The Persians invaded the country, but their large army was completely defeated by the Athenians, led by Miltiades, at the battle of Marathon, B.C. 490; and Darius died soon after.

Xerxes, the Ahasuerus of Scripture, succeeded to the vacant throne, and resumed the attack upon Greece. His immense army, like that assembled by Napoleon for the conquest of Russia, was composed of levies from the various states over which he exercised dominion. The entire armament is said to have amounted to more than two millions of combatants; and its progress appeared to be irresistible. At the pass of Thermopylæ, Leonidas, with his band of Spartans, arrested the advance of the Persian army, inflicting great losses upon it; but their resistance was at length overcome, and the Persians pursued their aggressive career. At Salamis, the Persian fleet sustained a calamitous defeat. It was dispersed, many of their ships having been destroyed, and the poet's description is not exaggerated:—

"A king sate on the rocky brow
Which looks o'er sea-born Salamis,
And ships by thousands lay below,
And men in nations—all were his;—
He counted them at break of day,
But when the sun set where were they?"

After this reverse, Xerxes fled into Persia,

and his army was again defeated, at Platæa. He was afterwards assassinated, and after his death no more powerful armaments were launched by Persia against Europe.

Greek mercenaries afterwards served against the Persian monarchs; and the adventures of some of these in the retreat of the ten thousand, the expedition of the younger Cyrus from Upper Asia, form the theme of Xenophon's "Anabasis." The glory of the kingdom declined, although the monarch was still the richest sovereign on the earth; and Darius III. or Codomanus verified the prediction of Daniel: "By his strength, through his riches, he shall stir up all nations against the realm of Grecia."—(Dan. xi. 2.) In exciting that country to make war upon Alexander, king of Macedonia, Darius III. aroused the indignation of that conqueror, who suddenly became the aggressor; and, B.C. 334, Persia was in its turn assailed. In that war the Persians were everywhere defeated; Darius III. was slain, and with him the old Persian empire expired. The successes of Alexander on the Granicus, at Issus, and at Arbela, sealed its fate; Greek colonies were founded in Asia, and for more than a century, the Persians groaned under the Grecian yoke. They then fell into vassalage under various nations, and in the third century of the Christian era, the famous Sassanian dynasty, which lasted more than four centuries, was founded. But the glory of the ancient kingdom had departed, and Persia never recovered her sceptre.

The luxurious style of living and the love of display for which the ancient Persians were celebrated are mentioned by many writers, sacred and profane. The testimonies of certain authors belonging to the latter class are quoted by Athenæus, in the twelfth book of his "Banquet of the Learned." He says: "But of all nations the Persians were the first to become notorious for their luxury; and the Persian kings even spent their winters at Susa, and their summers at Ecbatana. And Aristocles and Chares say that Susa derives its name from the seasonable and beautiful character of the place: for that what the Greeks call the lily is called in the Persian language σοῦσον. But they pass their autumns in Persepolis; and the rest of the year they spend in Babylon. And even the very thing which the Persian monarchs used to wear on their heads, showed plainly enough their extreme devotion to luxury. For it was made, according to the account of Dinon, of myrrh and of something called labyzus. And the labyzus is a sweet-smelling plant, and more valuable than myrrh. And whenever, says Dinon, the king dismounts from his chariot, he does not jump down, however small the height from the chariot to the ground may be, nor is he helped down, leaning on any one's hand, but a golden chair is always put by him, and he gets on that to descend; on which account the king's chair-bearer always follows him. And three hundred women are his guard, as Heraclides of Cumæ relates, in the first book of his history of Persia. And they sleep all day, that they may watch all night; and they pass the whole night in singing and playing, with lights burning.

"But Chares of Mitylene, in the fifth book of his 'History of Alexander,' says: 'The Persian kings had come to such a pitch of luxury, that at the head of the royal couch there was a supper-room laid with five couches, in which there were always kept five thousand talents of gold; and this was called the king's pillow. And at his feet was another supper-room, prepared with three couches, in which there were constantly kept three thousand talents of silver; and this was called the king's footstool. And in his bed-chamber there was also a golden vine, inlaid with precious stones, above the king's bed.' And this vine, Amyntas says in his 'Posts,' had bunches of grapes composed of most valuable precious stones; and not far from it there was placed a golden bowl, the work of Theodorus of Samos. And Agathocles, in the third book of his 'History of Cyzicus,' says that there is also amongst the Persians a water called the golden water, and that it rises in seventy springs; and that no one ever drinks of it but the king alone and the eldest of his sons. And if any one else drinks of it, the punishment is death.

"But Xenophon, in the eighth book of his 'Cyropædia,' says: 'They still used at that time to practise the discipline of the Persians, but the dress and effeminacy of the Medes.

But now they disregard the sight of the ancient Persian bravery becoming extinct, and they are solicitous only to preserve the effeminacy of the Medes. And I think it a good opportunity to give an account of their luxurious habits. For, in the first place, it is not enough for them to have their beds softly spread, but they put even the feet of their couches upon carpets, in order that the floor may not present resistance to them, but that the carpets may yield to their pressure. And as for the things which are dressed for their table, nothing is omitted which has been discovered before, and they are also continually inventing something new; and the same is the way with all other delicacies: for they retain men whose sole business it is to invent things of this kind. And in winter it is not enough for them to have their head, and their body, and their feet covered, but even on the tips of their fingers they wear shaggy gloves and finger-stalls; and in summer they are not satisfied with the shade of the trees and of the rocks, but they have also men placed in them to contrive additional means of procuring shade.'

"And in the passage which follows this one, he proceeds to say, 'But now they have more clothes laid upon their horses than they have even on their beds. For they do not pay so much attention to their horsemanship as to sitting softly. Moreover, they have porters, and bread-makers, and confectioners, and cup-bearers, and men to serve up their meals and to take them away, and men to lull them to sleep, and men to wake them, and dressers to anoint them and to rub them, and to get them up well in every respect.'"

In another part of this entertaining work—in which, amid much that is extravagant, frequently blemished by a freedom of expression that is found in most ancient authors, many pictures of ancient habits and modes of life are preserved—reference is made to the magnificence of the Persian banquets. Athenæus says (Book iv.), "But Heraclides the Cumæan, who compiled a history of Persia, in the second book of that work, which is entitled 'Preparatory,' says, 'And those who wait upon the Persian kings while they are at supper, all minister, after having bathed, wearing beautiful clothes; and they remain nearly half the day in attendance at the feast. But of those who are invited to eat with the king, some dine outside, and every one who chooses can see them, but some dine inside with the king: and even these do not actually eat with him; but there are two rooms opposite to one another, in one of which the king eats his meal, and in the other the guests eat theirs.

"And the king beholds them through the curtain which is at the door, but they cannot see him. But, sometimes, when there is a feast, then they all sup in one room, namely, in the same room as the king, being the large room. And when the king has a drinking party (and he has one very often), his guests are about a dozen in number; and when they have supped, the king by himself and his guests by themselves, then one of the eunuchs summons those who are to drink with the king: and when they come, then they drink with him, but they do not have the same wine; also they sit on the ground, and he reclines on a couch with golden feet; and when they are very drunk indeed, they go away. But for the most part, the king breakfasts and sups by himself: but sometimes his wife sups with him; and sometimes some of his sons do so. And at supper, his concubines sing and play to him; and one of them leads, and then all the rest sing in concert.

"But the supper," he continues, "which is called the king's supper, will appear to any one who hears of it to be very magnificent; still, when it is examined into, it will turn out to be economically and carefully managed, and in the same manner as the meals of the other Persians who are in office. For the king has a thousand victims slain every day: and amongst them are horses, and camels, and oxen, and asses, and stags, and an immense number of sheep; and a great many birds too are taken; and the Arabian ostrich (and that is a very large animal), and geese, and cocks; and a moderate quantity of them is served up to each of the mess-mates of the king, and each of them carries away what is left for his breakfast. But the greater part of these victims, and of this meat, is carried out into the court to the spear-bearers, and light-armed troops, whom the king maintains; and in the court, the masters of the feasts portion out the meat and the bread into equal portions; and as the mercenary troops in Greece receive money for their hire, so do these men receive food from the king, on account, as if it were money.

"And in the same way, at the courts of the other Persians, who hold office as magistrates, all the food is placed at once upon the table; and when the mess-mates of the magistrate have finished their supper, when he who superintends the meal distributes what is left on the table (and the greater part of the meat is left) to each of the servants. And each attendant, when he has received his share, has his food for the day. For the most honourable of the mess-mates never come to the king except to dinner; because, forsooth, they have requested permission not to be bound to come twice in the day, in order that they themselves may be able to receive guests at their own houses." Many more interesting particulars of this olden people are to be found in the works of the early classics, as well as in the sacred writings, and they all tend to show that the Persians, like most Asiastic nations, gradually abandoned their primitive simplicity, and plunged into an excess of luxury and extravagance.

Our brief account of ancient Persia would not be complete, if it did not contain some reference to their government and religion.

The form of government has always been that of a despotic sovereignty. The will of the monarch was law, and against his decrees there could be no appeal. The ceremonials of the court were tedious and stately, as many passages in the Book of Esther show; in fact, from all their subjects, from the highest to the lowest grades, the Persian despots exacted that absolute submission which characterizes the relations between ruler and people amongst Oriental nations.

The Persians are generally supposed to have been idolators, to have worshipped fire, and to have offered sacrifices to the sun and planets. These were probably at first venerated as symbols of the invisible God; and this species of worship gradually declined into idolatry. Sir W. Jones says:—" The primeval religion of Iran, if we may rely on the authorities adduced by Mohsan

Fani, was that which Newton calls the oldest of all religions—a firm belief that one supreme God made the world by His power, and continually governed it by His providence; a pious fear, love, and adoration of Him; a due reverence for parents and aged persons; a fraternal affection for the whole human species; and a compassionate tenderness even for the brute creation."

Every form of idolatry is believed by certain writers to be an imitation or a corruption of some system of revealed religion; and upon this principle the fire-worship of the Persians is traced to the miracle of God revealing Himself to Moses in the burning bush. Thus truth became deteriorated, and the manifestation of supreme power to one part of the human race was converted by others into an odious species of idolatry.

This system, which gradually assumed form and pressure amongst them, has been thus eloquently described by the author of "The Decline and Fall of the Roman Empire":—"The great and fundamental article of the system was the celebrated doctrine of the two principles; a bold and injudicious attempt of Eastern philosophy to reconcile the existence of moral and physical evil with the attributes of a beneficent Creator and Governor of the world. The first and original Being, in whom, or by whom, the universe exists, is denominated in the writings of Zoroaster, *Time without bounds;* but it must be confessed that this infinite substance seems rather a metaphysical abstraction of the mind than a real object endowed with self-consciousness, or possessed of moral perfections. From either the blind or the intelligent operation of this infinite Time, which bears but too near an affinity with the Chaos of the Greeks, the two secondary but active principles of the universe were from all eternity produced, Ormusd and Ahriman, each of them possessed of the powers of creation, but each disposed, by his invariable nature, to exercise them with different designs.

"The principle of good is eternally absorbed in light: the principle of evil eternally buried in darkness. The wise benevolence of Ormusd formed man capable of virtue, and abundantly provided his fair habitation with the materials of happiness. By his vigilant providence the motion of the planets, the order of the seasons, and the temperate mixture of the elements are preserved. But the malice of Ahriman has long since pierced *Ormusd's egg ;* or, in other words, has violated the harmony of his works. Since that fatal irruption, the most minute articles of good and evil are intimately intermingled and agitated together; the rankest poisons spring up amidst the most salutary plants; deluges, earthquakes, and conflagrations attest the conflict of Nature; and the little world of man is perpetually shaken by vice and misfortune. Whilst the rest of human kind are led away captives in the chains of their infernal enemy, the faithful Persian alone reserves his religious adoration for his friend and protector, Ormusd, and fights under his banner of light, in the full confidence that he shall, in the last day, share the glory of his triumph. At that decisive period the enlightened wisdom of goodness will render the power of Ormusd superior to the furious malice of his rival. Ahriman and his followers, disarmed and subdued, will sink into their native darkness; and virtue will maintain the eternal peace and harmony of the universe.

"The theology of Zoroaster was darkly comprehended by foreigners, and even by the far greater number of his disciples; but the most careless observers were struck with the philosophic simplicity of the Persian worship. 'That people,' says Herodotus, 'rejects the use of temples, of altars, and of statues, and smiles at the folly of those nations who imagine that the gods are sprung from, or bear any affinity with, the human nature. The tops of the highest mountains are the places chosen for sacrifices. Hymns and prayers are the principal worship; the Supreme God, who fills the wide circle of heaven, is the object to whom they are addressed.' Yet, at the same time, in the true spirit of a polytheist, he accuses them of adoring earth, water, fire, the winds, and the sun and the moon. But the Persians of every age have denied the charge, and explained the equivocal conduct which might appear to give a colour to it. The elements, and more particularly fire, light, and the sun, whom they called Mithra, were the objects of their religious reverence, because they considered them as the purest symbols, the noblest productions, and the most powerful agents of the divine power and nature.

"Every mode of religion, to make a deep and lasting impression on the human mind, must exercise our obedience by enjoining practices of devotion for which we can assign no reason; and must acquire our esteem by inculcating moral duties analogous to the dictates of our own hearts. The religion of Zoroaster was abundantly provided with the former, and possessed a sufficient portion of the latter. At the age of puberty the faithful Persian was invested with a mysterious girdle, the badge of the divine protection; and from that moment all the actions of his life, even the most indifferent or the most necessary, were sanctified by their peculiar prayers, ejaculations, or genuflexions; the omission of which, under any circumstances was a grievous sin, not inferior in guilt to the violation of the moral duties. The moral duties, however, of justice, mercy, liberality, &c., were, in their turn, required of the disciple of Zoroaster who wished to escape the persecution of Ahriman and to live with Ormusd in a blissful eternity, where the degree of felicity will be exactly proportioned to the degree of virtue and piety."

The Magi or sacerdotal order, gradually waxed numerous and powerful. They obtained possession of considerable property and wielded great influence. They were astrologers, and from them the Middle Age systems of that false science were derived. In fact, so much did their power increase that reform was rendered essential, and this was accomplished by Zerduscht, although the age in which he flourished cannot be fixed with any degree of precision. Of the Persian kings, the Magi, their antagonism, and the Zerduscht reformation, the Rev. F. D. Maurice, in his learned treatise on Moral and Metaphysical Philosophy, writes: "The Cyropædia, and the testimonies of Herodotus respecting the feelings of the Persians towards their king, and his inseparable connection with their worship, fully confirm another most important inference which we shall deduce from the legends respecting Zerduscht. The Magian, officially, was his antagonist; some *monarch* was always the ally in his reforms. To exalt the royal above the sacerdotal function, to prevent the kings from being the servants of the priests, was unquestionably a great part of his work. Herein he was probably acting out a faith which was far older in Persia than himself. It is difficult not to trace—most modern historians have traced—an opposition between the Persian and Median tribes (an opposition not preventing but necessitating an attempt at union between them) which points to more than the strife of mere personal feelings and interests.

"The Median predominance seems always to indicate the triumph of a priestly order and of priestly habits: the Persian prevalence shows that a king is ruling who knows that he is a king, and is determined to maintain his authority against all opposers, by whatever visible or invisible instruments they may work. The nobler kings, such as were Cyrus and Darius Hystaspes, do not merely proclaim their own tyranny. They assert that Ormusd is king; they are as entirely religious as those who are leagued against them; their faith is the ground of all their acts; in the strength of it they decree justice, organize satrapies, improve the tillage of the land, and constitute one of those mighty monarchies in which we recognize the character, strength, and spirit of Asia. In these monarchies everything depends upon the central power, or rather upon the earnestness with which the central power confesses its subjection to a gracious and beneficent Power, in whose name it rules and fights. The inscriptions which Major Rawlinson has recently interpreted, show how remarkably this was the case with Darius Hystaspes: they embody the very spirit of the Zerduscht reformation, and might almost tempt us to the notion—a favourite with some German critics (not, however, it seems to us, compatible with any of the popular traditions)—that he was identical with the Prophet. He no doubt realized the conception of the teacher much more than any mere teacher could have realized it. His order was that attempt to imitate the order of the heavenly bodies, the calmness and regularity of Nature, which one who looked upon light as the centre of the outward universe, and the king as the centre of the human society, would especially have admired and rejoiced in."

Such are the guesses at truth we have received respecting the history, religion, government, and manners and customs of the inhabitants of ancient Persia. It was one of the earliest principalities of the earth, and although the information to be obtained is not precise in its character, it is sufficient to justify the conclusion that Persia attained a high stage of civilization, and was the most important of those early dominions of the world.

CHAPTER II.

Changes and Vicissitudes in Persia in Modern Times.

For many centuries the Persians, who had so long ruled over other nations and tribes, fell under the dominion of more powerful states. The Greeks, as we have seen in the previous chapter, first obtained the ascendancy, which they wielded for about a century, and then the Parthians held them in vassalage for nearly five hundred years. At the expiration of that period Rome was gradually soaring to lofty destinies, and Parthia declining in power and importance. About A.D. 220, a successful soldier, Ardisheer Babigan, usually called Artaxerxes, wrested the sceptre from the feeble grasp of the Parthians, founded the celebrated Sassanian dynasty, which lasted nearly five centuries, and thus in a certain degree restored the Persian empire. Artaxerxes claimed to be descended from the ancient race of Persian monarchs, and assumed the title of "king of kings," but he is generally supposed to have sprung from parents of low origin. The reign of this sovereign and those of his successors in the Sassanian dynasty form the connecting link between the ancient and modern kingdoms of Persia. In the brilliant pages of Gibbon the reader will find a graphic summary of the long wars of this period between the Persians and Romans. The discord between the two empires was brought to a close A.D. 628, and, as the historian relates, "a war which had wounded the vitals of the two monarchies, produced no change in their external and relative situation."

The rulers of the Lower Empire turned every advantage to the best account, and the close of this long struggle did not constitute an exception in this respect. Gibbon relates (chap. xlvi.): "The return of Heraclius from Tauris to Constantinople was a perpetual triumph; and after the exploits of six glorious campaigns he peaceably enjoyed the sabbath of his toils. After a long impatience, the senate, the clergy, and the people went forth to meet their hero with tears and acclamations, with olive-branches, and innumerable lamps; he entered the capital in a chariot drawn by four elephants, and, as soon as the emperor could disengage himself from the tumult of public joy, he tasted more genuine satisfaction in the embraces of his mother and his son."

During the ascendancy of the Sassanian dynasty, Christianity was planted in Persia by the missionaries of Syria. It was violently opposed by the Magi, but after undergoing many vicissitudes and persecutions, it took deep root, and the Nestorians at one time obtained great power. Dissensions, however, continued to impede its progress, and, in the midst of these, Persia once more fell under a foreign yoke.

The first and most important event of modern history, is the sudden irruption of the Arabs, who, under the name of Saracens, conquered several Asiatic, African, and European states. One hundred years after the flight of Mahomed from Mecca the empire of his successors extended from India to the Atlantic ocean. The Persian monarchy, at that period in a declining condition, was the first to be attacked by the ambitious caliphs. The invasion of Persia (A.D.

632) by the Saracens proved disastrous; and after a severe repulse, on attempting to cross the Euphrates, they retired. They soon after returned to the assault, and gained a complete victory in the plains of Cadesia (A.D. 636). Similar results attended the battles of Jaloulah (A.D. 637) and Nehavend (A.D. 640), the latter being styled by the Saracens the "victory of victories," and the Sassanian dynasty was subverted. The ancient government and institutions of Persia, as well as the religion of Zoroaster, were overthrown, and the Persians compelled to embrace the faith of their Arab conquerors. The seat of the government was transferred to the new capital at Cufa, and Persia became a Saracen province.

As the power of the caliphs declined, Persia fell under the rule of the heads of powerful families, and many chiefs maintained themselves in various small principalities, and thus preserved at least a nominal independence amongst the people. To trace the career of the state under these various dynasties is hardly necessary. The rule of the sultans or monarchs of Ghizni, who obtained the sceptre

A.D. 961, appears to have been the most glorious. One of these, Sultan Mahmood, performed many brilliant achievements, and even extended his conquests to India. Having defeated the Hindoo prince Anundpal, who, with an immense army, had encamped near the Indus, Mahmood advanced boldly into India. In his progress he destroyed temples and idols, and on his return to Ghizni was received with great rejoicing and acclamation. Malcolm (vol. i. ch. ix.) states: "We are told by Eastern writers that on his return to Ghizni he celebrated a festival, at which he displayed to the admiring and astonished inhabitants of that city golden thrones magnificently ornamented, which had been constructed from the plunder of seven hundred maunds (each maund being not quite seven pounds' weight) of gold and silver plate, forty maunds of pure gold, two thousand maunds of silver, and twenty maunds of set jewels."

In his various expeditions into India Mahmood penetrated to Meerut, Delhi, Gwalior, and other places that have from recent events become the centre of public interest. His chief enterprise was for the destruction of the idol, Somnauth, then termed "the last refuge of idolatry."

An interesting account of the position and history of the temple of Somnauth is given in a note to Malcolm's "History of Persia" (vol. i. ch. ix.). The author says: "The temple stood in the county of Soreth, a province of the peninsula of Guzerat, which is now more generally known under the name of Kattywar; and which is celebrated in the Poorans for containing five inestimable blessings. First, the river Goomptee; second, beautiful women; third, good horses; fourth, Somnauth; and fifth, Dawarka. Among the many places in Soreth that are held sacred by the Hindoos, Somnauth, or Somnauth Putten as it is more generally termed, has always been one of the most remarkable. It stands one or two miles from the sea, at the junction of three rivers, the Hurna, Kupula, and Sersutty, at a distance of three miles to the east of the port of Belawul.

"Somnauth is one of the twelve symbols of Mahadeo, which are said to have descended from heaven to the earth. The great fame of this temple throughout the East attracted, as has been noticed, the bigotry and cupidity of Sultan Mahmood of Ghizni. The holy image was, according to Mahomedan authors, destroyed; but this fact is denied by Hindoos, who assert that the god retired into the ocean. The temple, though despoiled of its enormous treasures, soon recovered both fame and wealth sufficient to make it an object of attack to many Mahomedan princes; and Sultan Mahmood Begharah, who obtained possession of the throne of Amedabad in the year of the Hegirah, 877, marched against Somnauth, razed the temple to the ground, and, with the bigoted zeal of a Mahomedan conqueror, built a mosque upon the spot where it had stood. The province of Soreth has, ever since that period, remained under a Mahomedan government; but the persevering piety of the Hindoos has overcome the bigotry of their rulers. The mosque has fallen into ruin; and Ahsela Bhaee, the widow of a prince of the Mahratta family of Holkar, has lately erected a new temple on the exact site of that which was demolished. A symbol of Mahadeo has been placed in this temple, which is deemed peculiarly propitious to those who desire offspring; and Somnauth, though it has lost its former splendour, still retains its reputation, and is visited by pilgrims from every quarter, who pay a trifling duty to the Mahomedan ruler for the liberty they enjoy of paying their devotions at this favourite shrine.

"Not only the spot upon which the temple of Somnauth stands, but its vicinity, is celebrated in the tales of Hindoo mythology. It was on the plains near it on which the most celebrated battle of the Jadoos was fought. We are informed, that in this action, which took place about five thousand years ago, there were six crore, or sixty millions of combatants, and that all were slain. About a mile from Somnauth, at a place called Bhalka, the Hindoo pilgrim is shown a solitary peepul tree, on the bank of the Sersutty river, which he is assured stands on the exact spot where the god Shree Krishen received the mortal wound from an arrow that terminated his incarnation."

This celebrated idol Mahmood destroyed. Great treasures were found concealed in the hollow parts of the image, and these the conqueror seized and appropriated to his own use. This dynasty was brought to a close, A.D. 1160, in the person of Khoorsroo Malek, who was slain by a prince of the house of Ghour. The rule of the latter family was not of long duration, and for many years the empire was exposed to the assaults of various Tartar hordes, of which the Seljookee tribe long wielded the ascendancy. On the decline of the influence of this tribe the country fell under the rule of the Atta-begs, a number of petty princes or governors; Atta-beg being a Turkish word, compounded of *Atta*, master or tutor, and *beg*, lord; and signifies a governor, or tutor of a lord or prince.

During many ages the restless and wandering tribes that peopled the vast extent of country called Tartary had, under various appellations, burst upon the seats of empire and civilization, carrying death and destruction in their train. Led by some daring chief, these hardy races came into contact with the warriors of Rome, Greece, Persia, and the mighty hosts assembled for the Crusades. Gibbon states (chap. xxvi.): "In every age the immense plains of Scythia or Tartary have been inhabited by vagrant tribes of hunters and shepherds, whose indolence refuses to cultivate the earth, and whose restless spirit disdains the confinement of a sedentary life. In every age the Scythians and Tartars have been renowned for their invincible courage and rapid conquests. The thrones of Asia have been repeatedly overturned by the shepherds of the North, and their arms have spread terror and devastation over the most fertile and warlike countries of the earth."

Another irruption of these warrior races occurred in the commencement of the thirteenth century, when Persia was the first to fall under their attack. As these races exercised such influence upon the state of the world, and have entered so largely into the composition of modern nations, a short account of their origin, as it is related by Gibbon, will not be inappropriate. He says (chap. xxvi.), "The political society of the ancient Germans has the appearance of a voluntary alliance of independent warriors. The tribes of Scythia, distinguished by the modern appellation of *Hords*, assume the form of a numerous and increasing family, which, in the course of successive generations, has been propagated from the same original stock. The meanest and most ignorant of the Tartars preserve with conscious pride the inestimable treasure of their genealogy; and whatever distinctions of rank may have been introduced by the unequal distribution of pastoral wealth, they mutually respect themselves and each other as the descendants of the first founder of the tribe. The custom, which still prevails, of adopting the bravest and most faithful of the captives, may countenance the very probable suspicion that this extensive consanguinity is, in a great measure, legal and fictitious. But the useful prejudice which has obtained the sanction of time and opinion produces the effects of truth; the haughty barbarians yield a cheerful and voluntary obedience to the head of their blood, and their chief, or *mursa*, as the representative of their great father, exercises the authority of a judge in peace and of a leader in war. In the original state of the pastoral world, each of the *mursas* (if we may continue to use a modern appellation) acted as the independent chief of a large and separate family, and the limits of their peculiar territories were gradually fixed by superior force or mutual consent.

"But the constant operation of various and permanent causes contributed to unite the vagrant Hords into national communities, under the command of a supreme head. The weak were desirous of support, and the strong were ambitious of dominion; the power which is the result of union oppressed and collected the divided forces of the adjacent tribes; and as the vanquished were freely admitted to share the advantages of victory, the most valiant chiefs hastened to range themselves and their followers under the formidable standard of a confederate nation. The most successful of the Tartar princes assumed the military command, to which he was entitled by the superiority either of merit or of power. He was raised to the throne by the acclamations of his equals, and the title of *Khan* expresses in the language of the North of Asia, the full extent of the regal dignity.

"The right of hereditary succession was long confined to the blood of the founder of the monarchy; and at this moment all the Khans who reign from Crimea to the wall of China are the lineal descendants of the renowned Zingis. But as it is the indispensable duty of a Tartar sovereign to lead his warlike subjects into the field, the claims of an infant are often disregarded, and some royal kinsman, distinguished by his age and valour, is intrusted with the sword and sceptre of his predecessor. Two distinct and regular taxes are levied on the tribes, to support the dignity of their national monarch and of their peculiar chief; and each of those contributions amounts to the tithe both of their property and of their spoil.

"A Tartar sovereign enjoys the tenth part of the wealth of his people; and as his own domestic riches of flocks and herds increase in a much larger proportion, he is able plentifully to maintain the rustic splendour of his court, to reward the most deserving or the most favoured of his followers, and to obtain from the gentle influence of corruption the obedience which might be sometimes refused to the stern mandates of authority. The manners of his subjects, accustomed like himself to blood and rapine, might excuse in their eyes such partial acts of tyranny as would excite the horror of a civilized people, but the power of a despot has never been acknowledged in the deserts of Scythia. The immediate jurisdiction of the khan is confined within the limits of his own tribe, and the exercise of his royal prerogative has been moderated by the ancient institution of a national council.

"The Coroultai, or Diet of the Tartars, was regularly held in the spring and autumn, in the midst of a plain, where the princes of the reigning family and the mursas of the respective tribes may conveniently assemble on horseback with their martial and numerous trains, and the ambitious monarch who reviewed the strength must consult the inclination of an armed people. The rudiments of a feudal government may be discovered in the constitution of the Scythian or Tartar nations; but the perpetual conflict of those hostile nations has sometimes terminated in the establishment of a powerful and despotic empire. The victor, enriched by the tribute and fortified by the arms of dependent kings, has spread his conquest over Europe or Asia; the successful shepherds of the North have submitted to the confinement of arts, of laws, and of cities; and the introduction of luxury, after destroying the freedom of the people, has undermined the foundations of the throne."

As the Huns poured into Europe and swept away the ancient Roman dominion, so did the Moguls, led by Zingis Khan,* subvert the Persian and other empires. This mighty aggression is thus described by a modern historian:—"About the first years of the thirteenth century, the formidable name and victorious progress of a new conqueror and nation of Tartarian race first broke upon the astonished world. From the wide upland plains beyond the great Eastern desert, which extend to the Chinese wall, issued a race, described as countless in number, and as more horribly inhuman in aspect and spirit, and more utterly devoid of all civilization, than any of the destroyers of

* Properly Tchinggis Khakan.

mankind who had been let loose from the Tartarian regions to desolate the earth. Their earliest appearance in authentic history is under the general term of Moguls, and under the guidance of a leader whose proper designation of Temudgin has almost been lost in the national title, which was arrogated for his grandeur, of Zingis Khan, or the Mightiest of Lords. He was the son of a Khan who had reigned over thirteen hordes; and it is probable that the immense masses of the same generic features, who were drawn to his standard by the results of conquest or the thirst of rapine, derived their common term of Moguls from the original distinction of his own tribe.

"The early fortunes of a barbarian conqueror, the founder of his own greatness, are always obscure; the unlettered traditions of nomadic savages must be equally destitute of authenticity and interest; and we may at once dismiss the tale of vicissitudes, whether fabulous or real, which are ascribed to the youth of Zingis. He first burst the limits of his native Tartar region to precipitate his myriads upon the plains of China; the Great Wall proved but a feeble barrier against his innumerable cavalry; and after a desolating warfare, he tore five great provinces of the north from the huge but ill-cemented fabric of the Chinese dominion."

Such was the conqueror whom the Persians, at the commencement of the thirteenth century, rashly provoked. Zingis, indeed, is said to have been desirous of cultivating friendly relations with the Moslem princes, but an outrage provoked his ire and rendered war inevitable. A caravan consisting of three ambassadors and one hundred and fifty merchants, was attacked at Otrar, and the travellers murdered. This was said to have been done at the command of Mahomed, Sultan of Persia; and the Mogul ruler no sooner heard of the outrage than he vowed vengeance. His army amounted, it is said, to seven hundred thousand men. Four hundred thousand warriors led by the Persian Sultan, encountered this mighty host in the vast plains to the north of the Jaxartes, but after an obstinate struggle they were compelled to give way (A.D. 1217—1223). The chief cities of Persia were besieged and captured, and its richest and most populous provinces despoiled. The Sultan Mahomed retired to a desert island in the Caspian Sea, where, unpitied and alone, he soon after expired. His son, Geladeddin, made a gallant effort to change the fortunes of the war. Fighting step by step, as he retreated before the overwhelming forces of his assailant, he at last reached the banks of the Indus, when, in a moment of despair, he spurred his horse into the stream; and amid the acclamations of his opponents gained the other bank of the river in safety. Laden with the spoils of Persia, Zingis at length led his warriors back to their native plains, but did not long survive to enjoy the fruits of his numerous victories.

Soon after the death of this celebrated leader, the Moguls renewed their aggressions upon Persia. A series of struggles followed, the result of which was, that the Persians were completely subdued. Gelaleddin, who after his first gallant defence had resumed the Persian sovereignty, contended with more than ordinary valour, and fought fourteen great battles. His efforts were unavailing, and he ended his days in the mountains of Curdistan. The Moguls ruled over Persia about a century, but the influence of their chieftains gradually declined; Persia fell under the sway of a number of petty tyrants, whose power was crushed by Timour or Tamerlane, said to have been a descendant of Zingis Khan.

This warrior was born at the village of Sebzar, near Samarcand, and like so many of the conquerors whose career he imitated and whose glories he sought to rival, he carried his victorious standards into Persia and India. The former had, as we have seen, fallen under the rule of a number of petty tyrants, and its conquest was by no means difficult. The Persian forces gave way before the new assailant, and in a few years Timour had completely overrun the country (1380—1393). War was this chieftain's element, and he had no sooner subdued one state than he hastened to the attack upon another. After many campaigns he spent two months in relaxation at Samarcand, on which occasion he celebrated the marriage of six of his grandsons with extraordinary pomp and magnificence. His repose was not of long duration, and he set forward to invade China. The severity of the weather, and undue exertion, proved too much for his weakened frame, and he died of a fever in the seventieth year of his age (1405).

Gibbon sums up the effects of his sway in these words:—"The four following observations will serve to appreciate his claim to the public gratitude; and perhaps we shall conclude that the Mogul emperor was rather the scourge than the benefactor of mankind. 1. If some partial disorders, some local oppressions, were healed by the sword of Timour, the remedy was far more pernicious than the disease. By their rapine, cruelty, and discord, the petty tyrants of Persia might afflict their subjects; but whole nations were crushed under the footsteps of the reformer. The ground which had been occupied by flourishing cities was often marked by his abominable trophies—by columns or pyramids of human heads. Astracan, Carizme, Delhi, Ispahan, Bagdad, Aleppo, Damascus, Boursa, Smyrna, and a thousand others, were sacked or burned, or utterly destroyed in his presence and by his troops: and perhaps his conscience would have been startled if a priest or philosopher had dared to number the millions of victims whom he had sacrificed to the establishment of peace and order.

"2. His most destructive wars were rather inroads than conquests. He invaded Turkestan, Kipzak, Russia, Hindostan, Syria, Anatolia, Armenia, and Georgia, without a hope or a desire of preserving these distant provinces. From thence he departed laden with spoil; but he left behind him neither troops to awe the contumacious, nor magistrates to protect the obedient natives. When he had broken the fabric of their ancient government, he abandoned them to the evils which his invasion had aggravated or caused; nor were these evils compensated by any present or possible benefits.

"3. The kingdoms of Transoxiana and Persia were the proper field which he laboured to cultivate and adorn as the perpetual inheritance of his family. But his peaceful labours were often interrupted and sometimes blasted by the absence of the conqueror. While he triumphed on the Volga or the Ganges, his servants, and even his sons, forgot their master and their duty. The public and private injuries were poorly redressed by the tardy rigour of inquiry and punishment; and we must be content to praise the *Institutions* of Timour as the specious idea of a perfect monarchy.

"4. Whatsoever might be the blessings of his administration, they evaporated with his life. To reign, rather than to govern, was the ambition of his children and grandchildren,—the enemies of each other and of the people. A fragment of the empire was upheld with some glory by Sharokh, his youngest son; but after his decease, the scene was again involved in darkness and blood; and before the end of a century, Transoxiana and Persia were trampled by the Uzbeks from the North, and the Turkmans of the black and white sheep. The race of Timour would have been extinct, if a hero, his descendant in the fifth degree, had not fled before the Uzbek arms to the conquest of Hindostan. His successors (the great Moguls) extended their sway from the mountains of

Cashmir to Cape Comorin, and from Candahar to the gulf of Bengal. Since the reign of Aurungzebe their empire has been dissolved; their treasures of Delhi have been rifled by a Persian robber; and the richest of their kingdoms is now possessed by a company of Christian merchants of a remote island in the Northern Ocean."

At the beginning of the sixteenth century the Suffavean dynasty was established in Persia. About this time the Persians frequently came into collision with the Ottoman empire, then gradually rising into importance. Of this line of rulers, Shah Abbas, designated Shah Abbas the Great, who ascended the throne in 1585, was the most celebrated. He defeated the Usbegs, and in some degree restored the fortunes of the Persian empire. This powerful monarch received two Englishmen, Sir Anthony Sherley and his brother, on a mission, and showed a desire to enter into friendly relations with the European powers. He also put an end to the ravages of the Usbegs, established tranquillity in Persia, expelled the Turks from his territories, invited

Europeans to settle in his dominions, fostered commerce and encouraged learning. The noblest eulogy upon the character of Abbas, who died A.D. 1628, is contained in one short sentence, recorded by an impartial writer: "When this great prince ceased to live, Persia ceased to prosper."

The descendants of Abbas did not imitate his better qualities, and power soon fell from their grasp. The new masters of Persia were the Afghans, a collection of tribes inhabiting the mountainous tract of land between Khorassan and the Indus. Their origin has been a matter of much dispute. Some authorities assert that the name Afghan is derived from the Persian word signifying "lamentation;" and it was thus applied because these tribes bewailed their banishment from Judea. They are said to have been lineally descended from the Jewish captives carried off by Nebuchadnezzar. At an early date the Afghans were converted to the Mahomedan religion. Their country had long been subject to the conquerors of Persia and India, until their turn of triumph arrived, and for a season they wielded the sceptre over Persia. The appointment of Goorgeen Khan, prince of Georgia, to the government of Candahar led to a revolt (1704). This prince acted with great tyranny towards the Afghans, and even assailed the honour of the female branches of their ruling family. Meer Vais, the most powerful of the Afghan chiefs, dissembled his anger, and invited Goorgeen Khan to a sumptuous entertainment, at which he was murdered with all his attendants (A.D. 1709).

This was the signal for hostilities, in the course of which the Persians were defeated; and after a series of conflicts, Mahmood, son of Meer Vais, was proclaimed sovereign of Candahar (1717). At a great battle, fought under the walls of Ispahan (A.D. 1722), the Persians were again routed with loss, and their city was closely besieged. The Shah Hussein, having no alternative, attended by some of his nobles and three hundred of his troops, repaired to the Afghan camp in order to surrender. "His ungenerous enemy," says Malcolm, "could not refrain from insulting the fallen monarch; and the melancholy procession was commanded to halt within a short distance of the tents, on the pretext that Mahmood was asleep. After this delay, which would have been, according to the usage of the country, degrading to one of his subjects, he was at last permitted to proceed to the palace of Ferrâhâbâd, where he was introduced into a great hall, or saloon, in which he found his conqueror seated; and he had reached the centre of this room before the haughty Afghan rose to receive him. Hussein immediately addressed him in the following words: 'Son, since the great Sovereign of the universe does not will that I should reign any longer, and the moment has come which he has appointed for thy ascending the throne of Persia, I resign the empire to thee; may thy reign be prosperous!'

"After this speech he took the toorâh, or royal plume of feathers, from his turban, and gave it to the vizier of Mahmood; but that prince refused to accept it from any other but the monarch to whom it belonged. The meek Hussein rose, took it from the minister, and, while his arrogant enemy remained in his seat, he placed the rich emblem of royal power in his turban, and exclaimed, 'Reign in peace!' After the usual refreshments had been served, Mahmood deigned for the first time to speak to his captive. 'Such,' he observed, 'is the instability of human grandeur. God disposes of empires as he pleases—He takes them from one to give to another; but I promise ever to consider you as my father, and to undertake nothing without your advice.'" The Suffavean dynasty terminated with Hussein; for, although his son Tâmâsp assumed the title of king, the Persian empire passed, at least for a time, under the rule of the Afghans.

While Persia was involved in this struggle to preserve her independence, she was assailed by new enemies. The Russians, then just emerging from barbarism, invaded her territories in one direction, while the Turks attacked in another. Peter the Great had cast a longing eye upon the western shores of the Caspian; and he was not long in finding a pretext to justify his interference. The plunder of a Russian caravan on its way from

China was the assumed cause of this ruler's hostility. Peter put himself at the head of his army, sailed from the Volga, and reached the coast of Dâghestan. Having issued a proclamation, he took possession of Derbund (A.D. 1723). A treaty was afterwards concluded with Russia, by which it was stipulated that the czar should assist in expelling the Afghans and in establishing the Persian monarch on his throne, in return for which service the latter agreed to cede in perpetuity to Russia the towns of Derbund and Baku, with the provinces of Dâghestan, Shirwan, Ghilan, Mazenderan, and Asterabad.

While the Russians were assailing Persia to the north-west, the Turks entered Curdistan, and at first met with great success. The citizens of Tabreez worsted them; but, in a battle fought in 1725 the Persians met with a terrible defeat. A partition treaty of some of the finest provinces of Persia had been signed between the rulers of Russia and Constantinople. Thus, at this early period in their history, did the Russian Cæsars commence that policy which eventually brought them into collision with France and England. The treaty contained six articles. The share that fell to Russia was marked by a line that gave that state all the provinces on the Caspian from the country of the Turkomans to the confluence of the rivers Kur and Araxes. The portion intended for Turkey was bounded by a line which, commencing at that point, went by Tabreez, Hamadan, and Kermanshah, to Ardebil. The treaty was not, however, executed.

Soon after, Nâdir Kooli, a chief of great power and ability, born in Khorassan, obtained considerable celebrity, defeated the Afghans, and finally expelled them from Persia (1731). Thus terminated the Afghan invasion which had been the source of so much misery and such terrible calamities to the Persians. Their career had been one of destruction; and, although not powerful enough to retain possession of the conquest which they had made, they demolished some of the proudest public edifices, and despoiled the richest provinces of Persia.

Malcolm sums up the history of Persia from

the overthrow of the Sassanian dynasty in these words:—"The first enthusiasm of the religion of Mahomed had swept away the Sassanian dynasty; but a bold and able leader had, by the destruction of the Caliphs of Arabia, rescued his country from the ignominy of being deemed one of the provinces of another empire, and restored it to its dignity as a kingdom. From that period it had been in possession of Tartar chiefs, who had generally emigrated with their tribes into the milder climate of Persia, and whose power was continued for a time by the support of those warlike followers by whom it had been established. A revolution of a very uncommon nature had transferred the crown of Persia from these races of Tartar chiefs to the son of an ascetic.* Several of the first of the Suffavean princes were worthy of their exalted destiny; but the last century of the rule of this family presents us with a picture that can excite no feelings but those of disgust and indignation: and such was the debased and worthless character of some of these monarchs,

* Shah Ismail.

that the mind is almost reconciled to those dreadful scenes amid which they perished."

Persia once more relapsed into anarchy; powerful conquerors, like Nâdir Shah, could only for a time retrieve the fortunes of the empire, for everything bearing remote analogy to firm and permanent government had ceased.

Nâdir Shah belonged to the tribe of Affshâr, one of the seven Turkish tribes that had attached themselves to the family of the Suffavean dynasty. Nâdir was born of obscure parentage, in the province of Khorassan, A.D. 1688. He was at one time in the service of Shah Tâmâsp, and afterwards headed a band of robbers. Rewarded for some service against the Usbegs, he became a chief of great reputation, and gradually rose in distinction. The design of usurping the supreme power soon entered into this ambitious chieftain's mind, and the weakness of the character of Tâmâsp favoured this scheme. Nâdir, "like Ardisheer, the founder of the Sassanian race of kings, had his visions of future grandeur. He saw, we are told, in one of these, a water-fowl and a white fish with four horns: he dreamt that he shot the bird; and, after all his attendants had failed in their attempts to seize the extraordinary fish, he stretched out his hand and caught it with the greatest ease. The simple fact of his dreaming of a bird and a fish, he was informed by flattering astrologers, was a certain presage of his attaining imperial power; and his historian has had a less difficult task in discovering, from subsequent events, that the four horns of the fish were types of the kingdoms of Persia, Khaurizm, India, and Tartary, which were all destined to be conquered by this hero."

In 1730, Nâdir received a grant of four provinces. Having vanquished the Afghans, he marched against the Turks, with whom the Shah Tâmâsp concluded an inglorious peace (A.D. 1732), which furnished Nâdir with the opportunity he desired; and the reigning monarch was soon after deposed. After some delay, Nâdir mounted the vacant throne (A.D. 1736). The manner in which this was accomplished was peculiar, and in some respects resembles that passage in our own history in which the elevation of Richard the Third is recorded.

The infant heir to the Persian throne died at Ispahan; and some authors assert that the child was put to death by Nâdir's orders. The ambitious chieftain assembled the principal nobles and officers at a banquet, at the festival of the Nouroze or vernal equinox, and spoke to them in these terms:—"Shah Tâmâsp and Shah Abbas were your kings, and the princes of their blood are the heirs to the throne. Choose one of them for your sovereign or some other person whom you know to be great and virtuous. It is enough for me that I have restored the throne to its glory, and delivered my country from the Afghans, the Turks, and the Russians."

Having made this speech, Nâdir retired while the nobles deliberated, but he was soon recalled to have the crown offered for his acceptance. This the wily chieftain pretended to reject, and we are told that the same scene was acted daily for a month. At last his assumed reluctance gave way, but he demanded the suppression of a powerful religious sect as the price of his assent. Nâdir said, "I must insist that, as I sacrifice so much for Persia, the inhabitants of that nation shall, in consideration for one who has no object but their tranquillity, abandon that belief which was introduced by Shah Ismail, the founder of the Suffavean dynasty, and once more acknowledge the authority of the first four caliphs. Since the schism of Sheah has prevailed, this country has been in continual distraction: let us all become Soonees, and that will cease. But, as every national religion should have a head, let the holy Imaum Jaaffer, who is of the family of the prophet, and whom we all venerate, be the head of ours." The request was of course complied with, and Nâdir accepted the sovereignty.

This powerful sovereign gained many victories over various enemies, and conquered India; but at his death the reins of authority fell into weak hands, and the fortunes of the Persian monarchy again declined. Only under the rule of Kurreem Khan (A.D. 1759—1779) did the empire enjoy a temporary prosperity. It often happened that various competitcrs struggled for ascendancy, and the regular succession was altogether broken up.

Sir J. Malcolm says:—"The extraordinary rise of Nâdir Shah and of Kurreem Khan had destroyed that sacred regard for the royal family which had so powerfully protected the weakest of the Suffavean monarchs. Every leader who had followers thought that chance might give him the crown. The usurpation of the name of king was so common, that the title was no longer held in respect; and men, amid the continual change of rulers, had lost their habits of obedience to the only paramount authority that was recognized by the usages of the country. This is no overcharged picture: and it may be affirmed that when the success of Aga Mahomed Khan obtained him the rule of Persia, that kingdom was in a state of complete anarchy. The chiefs of the principal tribes cherished plans of inordinate ambition. Their followers, accustomed to scenes of revolt and of plunder, were adverse to any power which deprived them of their harvest of spoil. The towns and villages had been pillaged so often, that many of their inhabitants, compelled to abandon their homes, sought relief in the practice of that violence by which they had been ruined; while others became voluntary exiles from their country. Commerce had gradually declined; for, independent of the hazards which merchants incurred from the upstart rulers of the day, the public roads were infested by plunderers who seized upon all property that they found unguarded."

Aga Mahomed Khan, the founder of the reigning family, rescued many of the fairest provinces of Persia from the grasp of the aggressor, and in 1796 accepted the crown. For many years before, he had virtually governed Persia, and in some measure restored the glories and importance of the kingdom. His life was cut off by assassins in 1797, and the sceptre has since been wielded by his descendants, some of whom have given evidence of the possession of considerable ability.

During the years of the decline of the Persian monarchy, Russia has taken every advantage of its weakness for purposes of self-aggrandizement. As we have seen, Peter the Great formed plans for its partition; and

Catherine faithfully adhered to this policy. Catherine II. invaded Persia; but the Russian army was recalled just as Aga Mahomed Khan had put himself at the head of the Persian forces. Death terminated his victorious career, and under the rule of his successor the attack was renewed. Georgia and other provinces were wrested from Persia. In January, 1814, a treaty between Russia and Persia was published at St. Petersburg, in which the latter power ceded a number of governments on the Caspian Sea and the whole of Dâghestan; it also renounced all claims to Georgia, Immeritia, Guria, and Mingrelia, and ceded them in full sovereignty to Russia.

These concessions did not, however, satisfy the rapacity of the czars. Under various pretences they sought to despoil Persia, to obtain an undue ascendancy over her monarchs, and to make the possession of that country the vantage ground for assailing the dominion of the British in India. The late Czar Nicholas had no sooner settled himself upon the throne of his ancestors, and completed the necessary preparations, than he made war upon Persia.

Some disputes, having reference to the boundary line between the two empires, afforded the pretext for this new aggression. In this war Persia was of course defeated, and the Russian despots further reduced the territories of this power. The treaty of peace was concluded at Tourkmantchai, on the 28th of February, 1828, and it is thus described in the Annual Register of that year:—"By this treaty, Persia gave up to Russia the whole Khanat of Erivan, on both sides of the Araxes, and the Khanat of Nakhitchevan, which thus brought Russia creeping onwards still further south. But this was not all. Along the most southerly part of this frontier the Araxes was now declared to be the boundary. But on this part of the Araxes was the strong fortress of Abbas Abad, and, unfortunately for Russia, it stood on the right bank of the river. Persia, therefore, was compelled to cede the fortress, too, with three wersts and a half of the surrounding country. Persia farther agreed to pay the sum of 20,000,000 rubles, and consented that, while both powers should have the navigation of the Caspian for commercial purposes, Russia alone should be entitled to keep vessels of war upon it. She further accorded an amnesty to such inhabitants of Adzerbidjan as had espoused the cause of Russia, allowing them to emigrate into Russia if they should be so inclined, and granting them, for that purpose, one year in which to dispose of their movable property, and five years to dispose of their lands. Russia, in return, recognized the crown prince, Abbas Meerza, as heir-apparent of the Persian crown. In the policy of Russia there is nothing more insidious than her practice of first stirring to rebellion provinces of the countries which she invades, and then stipulating for a pardon to their rebellion when she makes peace. The population of these provinces (and they are always frontier provinces) come to regard her as a protector; she acquires a right to take care that the indemnity is duly observed. Rebels pardoned by compulsion are never treated with kindness; and their protector can never be at a loss for complaints of violations of treaty to serve as pretexts for a war whenever he shall wish one."

No sooner had Russia concluded peace with Persia, than her arms were turned against Turkey. The overthrow of both of these states has long been the cherished object of her rulers. The violent manner in which the late czar sought to carry out his aggressive policy against Turkey brought France and England to the rescue. Of the Ottoman empire Nicholas also wished to play the part of the protector, but the monstrous iniquity of the proceeding was detected, and the independence of Europe preserved. Russia, however, keeps pressing upon Persia; and her triumph at Kars caused her power and importance to be greatly exaggerated amongst the Asiatic nations; but it is to be hoped that she will not again be permitted to despoil her weaker neighbour, and to break down this barrier power which interposes between her dominions and those of England in Asia.

CHAPTER III.

Differences between England and Persia.

Titles and outward demonstrations are matters of vast importance in the eyes of the Persian sovereigns and their subjects. In fact, all the stateliness of Asiatic ceremonial is still preserved in this country, although it has long since declined from its position as a dominant or even a first-rate power. The shadow of authority is retained, but the substance has been lost. In the preamble of a treaty between England and Persia, concluded with Colonel Malcolm, at the commencement of the present century we find the Persian monarch thus described: — "The high king, whose court is like that of Solomon's, the asylum of the world, the sign of the power of God, the jewel in the ring of kings, the ornament in the cheek of eternal empire, the grace of the beauty of sovereignty and royalty, the king of the universe like Caherman, the mansion of mercy and justice, the phœnix of good fortune, the eminence of never-fading prosperity, the king powerful as Alexander, who has no equal among the princes exalted to majesty by the heavens in this globe, a shade from the shade of the Most High, a prince before whom the sun is concealed."

Weak monarchs, ruling over declining states, but too often entertain extravagant notions respecting their own power and importance; and many unseemly squabbles, having reference to court etiquette and the treatment and bearing of the ambassadors of friendly powers, are the result. Disputes of this character, and the designs of Persia upon certain portions of Afghanistan, have for many years tended to estrange the British and Persian governments.

Persia may be regarded as one barrier of our East-Indian dominions; and the rulers of Russia, aware of this fact, have availed themselves of every opportunity for creating a difficulty between the two states. Every advance made by Persia towards India is a step gained by Russia. Her settled policy has been to seek, by all possible means, to induce the Persian monarch to pursue an unbecoming and offensive course in his dealings with England; and whether the treatment of the British representatives in Persia, or the occupation of Herat, was the point in debate, Russian diplomatists have invariably sought to aggravate the case and render an accommodation impossible. These grievances are of long standing, and to understand the matter aright, we must turn our attention to the designs of Persia against the independence of Afghanistan.

The kingdom of Afghanistan, as most of our readers know, has long formed the great bulwark of British India upon the Asiatic side. It was the high road to conquest in India for many ages, until the English and other nations approached the coveted possession from the sea. The chief passes of this barrier land admit of easy access from the Persian dominions, and Russia is fully aware that while this state is preserved in its integrity it must prove an obstacle to the accomplishment of her designs against India. Hence her efforts have been to produce complications in that quarter, and these have frequently been crowned with success.

In the new edition of the "Encyclopædia Britannica" Afghanistan is thus described:— "The boundaries of Afghanistan have fluctuated with the vicissitudes of war from the middle of the tenth century, when the Turkish slave Alptegin first founded the dynasty of Ghuzni, to the date of the recent invasion of the country by the British. At the latter period, the kingdom consisted of four subdivisions, Cabul, the Huzareh country, Candahar, and Herat. Taken in this extent, Afghanistan is bordered on the north by Bokhara, Kunduz, and Kaferistan; on the east by the British province of Peshawur and the Soliman range of mountains; on the south by Beloochistan; and on the west by Persia. Its greatest length from north to south is about six hundred miles; its breadth measures about the same distance. The Afghans have no general name for their country but that of Afghanistan, which, Mr. Elphinstone thinks, was probably first employed in Persia. It is frequently used in books, and is not unknown to the inhabitants. It is sometimes known under the appellation of the kingdom of Cabul."

This extensive tract of country is inhabited by a number of tribes, subdivided into clans; and amongst them the old patriarchal form of government is in a great measure retained. The chief of a tribe is called a Khan; and at certain periods in their history some ambitious chieftain has collected the various tribes under his banner and led them to conquest. Thus, as we have seen in a former chapter, Persia itself was at one time under the rule of the Afghans.

Afghan, in the native traditions, is said to have been the son of Irmia or Birkia, son of Saul, the Israelitish king. To descend, however, from the unauthenticated traditions of the people to the fairer domains of history, we find that a Tartar officer named Sebuctaghi, who had married the daughter of Alptegin, conquered Afghanistan, and was acknowledged as Alptegin's successor. His son Mahmood pursued the career of conquest, and extended the Afghan empire over Cabul, India, Balkh, Badukshan, and a great part of Khorassan. This dynasty was, A.D. 1159, succeeded by that of Ghor, which terminated in 1206. Zingis Khan and Timour overran the country; and on the fall of the Mogul empire in India, the plains of Afghanistan were divided between Persia and Hindostan.

During these reverses the native Afghan tribes took refuge in their mountains. On the decline of the power of those by whom they had been expelled from their country, they once more descended into their native plains, and after undergoing a variety of vicissitudes, and maintaining a long struggle with their numerous assailants, Ahmed Shah, an officer of the Dooraunee tribe, founded the modern Afghan kingdom. This warlike prince invaded Hindostan, and in 1773 left the empire which he had founded to his son Timour. The latter proved himself but an unworthy successor of so distinguished a parent, and after his death in 1792, the kingdom became the scene of civil contention. Timour's sons quarrelled over the heritage, rival chieftains stepped in, and in

1833 the only portion of this once powerful state that remained under the rule of a descendant of its founder was the town and principality of Herat.

For some years Prince Kamran of Herat had been in the habit of sending an occasional tribute to the shah of Persia, without directly acknowledging his supremacy. The successes of Abbas Meerza, the prince royal, in his Khorassan campaigns, rendered Prince Kamran still more submissive. Abbas Meerza died in 1833, and in the same year his father, Futteh Ally Shah, sovereign of Persia, also expired, and his grandson, Mahomed Shah, ascended the Persian throne. These changes led to serious results. Prince Kamran refused to ratify his previous engagements, and a misunderstanding arose between him and the Persian sovereign. In a despatch to Lord Palmerston, dated December 30, 1835, Mr. Ellis, who had been sent on a mission of condolence and congratulation to the young shah, stated the case in these words:—"Herat and some neighbouring districts are under the immediate authority of Kamran Meerza, whose father,

Mahmood Shah, was for a short time king of Cabul. Kamran Meerza, without directly acknowledging the sovereignty of Persia, has been in the habit of paying annually a sum of money to the shah of Persia whenever the governor of Khorassan, the province of Persia adjacent to Herat, was in a condition to threaten an attack upon Kamran Meerza's principality. The successes of Abbas Meerza in his Khorassan campaigns, led to the contracting of certain engagements on the part of Kamran Meerza, the principal of which were the razing of the fort of Ghorian, the return of certain families to their domicile in Persia, and the payment of a sum of ten thousand tomauns annually to the shah. The Herat prince has failed in the performance of all, and the shah has consequently a right to obtain redress by force of arms. Under such circumstances, even if the British government was not restrained by the ninth article* of the existing

* Treaty of Nov. 25, 1814. Art. IX.—If war should be declared between the Afghans and Persians, the English Government shall not interfere with either party, unless their mediation to effect a peace shall be solicited by both parties.

treaty from interfering between the Persians and Afghans, it would be difficult to oppose an attack upon Herat, or to define the exact limit to which hostilities were to be carried against Kamran Meerza; but an attempt to annex Candahar and Ghizni to the Persian dominions, upon pretensions derived from the time of Nâdir Shah, has no such justification, and could not be looked upon with indifference by the British Government."

Such is the account given by an agent of the British Government of the state of this question in 1835. At that time the English representatives in Persia were seeking by all means in their power to induce the young shah to abstain from an attack upon Herat, and to endeavour to obtain redress by means of negotiation; whilst Count Simonich, the Russian minister at the court of Teheran, advised him to embark at once in a career of conquest. In the following year, this policy was advocated with greater earnestness, and Count Simonich recommended the immediate prosecution of the enterprise, on the plea, that what could then be effected with ten thousand men, would not in the following year be practicable with a much larger number.

The Parliamentary papers in which these transactions are related contain some very important disclosures with reference to the real character of Russian diplomacy, and show that the same pernicious system of deception, propounded by the Czar Nicholas to Sir G. H. Seymour at St. Petersburg, is carried out in every branch of the diplomatic service of that state. The policy advocated by Count Simonich was so much at variance with the professed principles and the declared system of the Russian Government, that Lord Palmerston, in 1837, wrote to the Earl of Durham, at that time ambassador at St. Petersburg, to bring the matter under the attention of the Russian Government. This was done, and Count Nesselrode replied, that our minister must have been misinformed, as Count Simonich had been distinctly ordered to dissuade the shah from prosecuting the war at any time and in any circumstances. But it was a well-known fact, that Count Simonich not only urged the advance of the Persians against

Herat, but actually offered his services to the shah in a military capacity. So much for the truthfulness of Russian diplomacy.

While England was doing all in her power to prevent, and Russia was seeking to precipitate a contest, Uzeez Khan, an Afghan nobleman of rank, arrived at Tehran from Kohundil Khan, Rahmdil Khan, and Sheerdil Khan, the brother chiefs of Candahar, on a mission to the shah. The object of this advance was to obtain an alliance, offensive and defensive, against Prince Kamran of Herat. This envoy was favourably received, the terms of the alliance were accepted, and preparations made for an immediate advance. Two expeditions were accordingly prepared in 1836, the one to chastise the Turkomans and Oosbegs who had then lately committed depredations in Asterabad and the neighbouring districts, and another against Herat. The shah set forth at the head of his troops, which by the commencement of the winter of 1836 had proceeded no further than Asterabad. The appearance of the cholera in Khorassan, scarcity of provisions, and the incursions of predatory foes, compelled the shah to abandon the design of a winter campaign against Herat; and, much to the disgust of the Russian minister, the Persian forces retired. Previous to their withdrawal, the shah made an attempt to negotiate, and received the following answer:—

"You demand hostages. We gave no hostages during the reign of the late shah, and we will give none now. You demand a present: we are ready to give as large a present as we can afford. If the shah is not satisfied with this, and is determined to attack us, let him come. We will defend our city as long as we can; and if we are driven from it, it will of course remain in your hands till we can find means to take it back again from you."

In the first instance the prince and people of Herat were clearly in the wrong. This was admitted by Mr. Ellis; and his successor, Mr. McNeill (afterwards Sir John McNeill), expressed a similar opinion. He says, in a despatch dated Tehran, February 24, 1837: "Putting aside the claims of Persia to the sovereignty of Herat, and regarding the question as one between two independent sovereigns, I am inclined to believe that the government of Herat will be found to have been the aggressor. On the death of Abbas Meerza, when the present shah returned from his unsuccessful expedition against Herat, negotiations were entered into, which terminated in the conclusion of an agreement for a cessation of hostilities between the parties, and the demarcation of a line of boundary. From that time up to the present moment, Persia has committed no act of hostility against the Afghans; but on the death of the late shah the government of Herat made predatory incursions into the Persian territories, in concert with the Turkomans and Huzarehs, and captured the subjects of Persia for the purpose of selling them as slaves. This system of warfare has from that time been carried on without intermission by the Afghans of Herat, and Persia has not retaliated these acts of aggression by any hostile measure—unless the public annunciation of its intention to attack Herat should be regarded as such. Under these circumstances, there cannot, I think, be a doubt that the shah is fully justified in making war on Prince Kamran: and though the capture of Herat by Persia would certainly be an evil of great magnitude, we could not wonder if the shah were to disregard our remonstrances, and to assert his right to make war on any enemy who has given him the greatest provocation, and whom he may regard himself as bound in duty to his subjects to punish, or even to put down."

Early in 1837 preparations were made for another expedition against Herat. Whilst these were in progress, an envoy, Futteh Mahomed Khan, arrived at Tehran, bringing proposals from Prince Kamran for an amicable settlement of the dispute. Mr. McNeill was invited to the conference assembled to consider these offers, which were as follows:—

"1. There is to be a cessation of war and of marauding; the capture and sale of prisoners are to be utterly abolished. 2. Should the King of Kings intend to undertake a military expedition against Toorkistan, and should he require troops from Shah Kamran, the latter is to supply troops to the extent of his ability, and they shall accompany the governor of Khorassan on any expedition against Toorkistan. Should troops be required on the frontiers of Azerbijan, Shah Kamran shall furnish them in such number as may at the time be practicable, and shall not withhold them. 3. A sum of money, in the shape of tribute, shall be paid annually, at the festival of Noorooz, to the Persian government. 4. Merchants from every quarter, who shall arrive in the territories of Herat and its dependencies, are to receive full protection and suffer no injury in person or property. 5. One person, who shall be a descendant of Shah Kamran, and some other persons who shall be relations of Vizier Yar Mahomed Khan and of Sheer Mahomed Khan, shall reside for two years at Meshed as hostages. When the period of two years has elapsed, if the ministers of Herat shall have performed the foregoing engagements, and shall have committed no infraction, the above hostages shall be despatched to Herat, and shall not be detained more than two years. Should any infraction of the above engagements have been committed, the hostages are to be retained until the time of their fulfilment. 6. A vakeel, or agent, from Shah Kamran shall always reside at the court of the King of Kings.

"I engage for the performance of the foregoing stipulations on the part of my master, Shah Kamran, on condition that the following engagements shall be agreed to:—

"1. The King of Kings of Persia shall consider Shah Kamran as his brother, and treat him with regard. 2. The ministers of the King of Kings of Persia shall not interefere in any manner whatever in the succession of the posterity of Shah Kamran. Whichever of the descendants of Shah Kamran shall succeed him in his government and titles, and shall fulfil the engagements that have been here contracted, it is stipulated on the part of the King of Kings of Persia that these engagements shall continue in full force, and shall not undergo any alteration. 3. Troops are not to be sent into the territories in the possession of Shah Kamran; war and marauding are to cease; and the capture and sale of prisoners are to be entirely abolished. The government of the King of Kings of Persia is not to interfere in any manner whatever in the internal affairs of the territories in the possession of Shah Kamran; and to enable the government of Herat to fulfil its engagements, the internal management of these territories is to be entirely under the control of the government of Herat. 4. The English government shall be mediators between the Persian and Herat governments; and if there should be any infraction of these engagements by either party, it shall employ every exertion to obtain their fulfilment."

From the moment the government of Herat made this advance the character of the contest was entirely changed. Russia was evidently checkmated, and Persia, acting under her sinister influence, refused to accept these concessions. In fact, it became evident that not reparation, but the acquisition of Herat, was the object of the Persian monarch. The Persian prime minister, in his rejection of the terms of accommodation, declared Herat and its dependencies to be one of the provinces of Persia. On the 23rd of July, 1837, the Persian army set out upon its march, and was, on the 10th of October, joined by Captain Vicovich, who publicly announced that he was sent forward to give notice of the speedy arrival at Asterabad of a large Russian force intended to co-operate with the army against Herat. Various intrigues were carried on with the various rulers of Afghanistan, both by Persia and Russia, but these do not fall within the scope of our subject.

The Persian army continued its march in spite of the remonstrances of the British minister. Ghorian fell after a siege of ten days; and early in December Herat was besieged. All attempts at negotiation failed—the shah demanding that Kamran should present himself at the Persian camp to tender his submission and surrender the place; while the government of Herat, on the other hand, refused to conclude any treaty till the shah should have retired to Meshed. The defence was gallantly maintained; and Mr. McNeill wrote, on the 23rd of February, 1838:—"The defence which Herat has made is very creditable to its inhabitants; and, considering the amount of the means which the shah succeeded in collecting before it (nearly forty thousand men and eighty guns), the want of artillery in the town, the facility with which his majesty has obtained supplies, the depressing effect upon the Heratees of the fall of Ghorian, the failure of all their allies to afford them efficient succour, and the unusual mildness of season so favourable to the operations of a siege—I confess the value of Herat has been greatly enhanced in my estimation; and, although I have always regarded it as a most important position with reference to the security and tranquillity of India, I was not prepared to look on it as so strong and defensible a place, or as one so capable of being made a barrier to the advance of any hostile power; and I feel that, if Herat should fall into the hands of any such power, it would be an evil even greater than I had hitherto believed it would be." These considerations induced Mr. McNeill to advise the English government to interfere for the preservation of the independence of this important fortress.

In the mean time other matters calculated

to embroil the two countries had arisen. A gholan, or confidential messenger, one Ali Mahomed Beg, who had been sent by Mr. McNeill to attend upon the envoy of Herat, was, on his return in October, 1837, while bearing missives for the British minister, seized and maltreated. "When within about three stages of Meshed," says Mr. McNeill in his report, "after he had already passed the Persian army, then marching to Toorbut Sheikh Jaum, the caravan which Ali Mahomed Beg accompanied was met by Mr. Borowski, who had been some time in the Persian service, and who was then on his way from Meshed to join the camp. Mr. Borowski having recognized the man (who was travelling openly and without disguise or concealment, accompanied by two horses and a pony besides the horse he rode), and having learnt that he was returning from Herat, reported the circumstance on his arrival in camp. Horsemen were immediately despatched to bring the messenger to camp. He was forced to return with them; a part of his clothes were taken from him; the horses which he was bringing for me from Herat were seized; he was dragged to camp, and there placed in custody. He succeeded, however, in making his way to the tent of Colonel Stoddart, and was by that officer conducted to the prime minister, who, after he had been informed by Colonel Stoddart that the man was in the service of this mission, again placed him in custody; while Hajee Khan, an officer of the rank of brigadier in the service of the shah, not only used offensive language in addressing Colonel Stoddart in presence of the prime minister, but, after the messenger had been released by order of his excellency, seized him again in the midst of the camp, stripped him to search for any letters he might have concealed about his person, took from him Lieutenant Pottinger's letter (which was sent to the prime minister), used to the messenger the most violent threats and the most disgusting and opprobious language, and took from him a portion of his accoutrements. The prime minister, having received Lieutenant Pottinger's letter to me, sent for Meerza Sauleh, one of the Persian gentlemen who was educated in England, and directed him to open and read the letter; but the Meerza declined to open the letter. The letter was, therefore, returned unopened."

For this outrage, Mr. McNeill demanded an apology from the prime minister for the share taken by him in the transaction, and the punishment of Hajee Khan for the personal violence inflicted by him on Ali Mahomed Beg.

The other offence, of the commission of which the British representative in Persia complained, was of a serious character. In December, 1837, an Indian dervish, apparently under the influence of bhang (an intoxicating drug which the Indians are in the habit of smoking), without any provocation made use of insulting language to Mr. Gerald, the apothecary attached to the British residency at Bushire, and also knocked off his cap. Mr. Gerald retaliated by kicking his assailant. In consequence of this retaliation, the syud, a descendant of the prophet, was said to have received such injuries as to be in a dying state. The Mahomedans demanded that Mr. Gerald should be delivered into their hands; and the governor of Bushire actually threatened a repetition of what had occurred at the Russian embassy in Tehran on a similar occasion.* It was soon ascertained that the syud had received but little injury; and he afterwards armed himself with a hatchet, determined, as he declared, to obtain his object by assaulting some of the people of the British residency. Fortunately no evil results accrued from these violent and illegal proceedings, but satisfaction was at once demanded. Of course these matters only tended to widen the breach between the two countries. The energetic prosecution of the siege of Herat by the Persian government had produced an estrangement aggravated by these indignities offered to British subjects.

Russia kept urging the shah forward in his

* In February 1829, a dispute having arisen between the populace of Tehran and the Russian mission, the former attempted to force an entrance into the Russian minister's house, in order to rescue two persons supposed to be forcibly detained there. The Russian servants fired upon and killed one of the mob, whereupon the populace broke into the house and put to death the minister himself and every Russian subject in his suite except one.

desperate career. Captain Vicovich reached the camp on the 10th of October, and soon after repaired to Cabul, and by a tortuous diplomacy endeavoured to increase the embarrassment. At Candahar, the efforts of the Russian agents were crowned with more success; and on the 11th of April, 1838, Mr. McNeill forwarded to the British government the following copy of the draft of a treaty between the chief of Candahar and the Persian monarch, under the sealed guarantee of the Russian ambassador at Tehran:—" I, as minister plenipotentiary of the Russian government at the court of Persia, guarantee the fulfilment of the following conditions of treaty between his majesty Mahomed Shah, and the sirdar of Candahar. 1. The principality of Herat to be bestowed by the shah on the rulers of Candahar, as a reward for their faithful services performed to him since his accession to the throne of Persia. 2. The territories and tribes at present subject to the sirdars of Candahar to be preserved to them free of violence, injury, or confiscation. 3. The Persian government in no way to amalgamate with their own subjects any of the Afghan tribes, great or small, nor to employ them upon service unconnected with their own affairs; and all business relative to the Afghan states to be submitted by the Persian government to the rulers of Candahar. 4. The Prince Kamran and his minister, Yar Mahomed Khan, to be excluded from all participation in the councils of Persia. 5. Should any hostile movement be made against Candahar by Shooja-ool-Molk, the English, or the ameer of Cabul, aid to be afforded by the shah to the sirdars. 6. In the event of the sons or brothers of Kahundil Khan coming with an auxiliary force to the royal camp, no violence or injury to be in any way offered to the persons or property of them or their followers, and none of them to be detained as hostages, with the exception of a single son of Kohundil Khan's, who will always remain in the service of the shah. 7. A contingent of twelve thousand horse and twelve guns to be supplied by the Candaharees, to garrison Herat—receiving pay and rations from them, and to assist the shah on occasion of service. 8. On the arrival of the treaty duly ratified at Candahar, Mahomed Omar Khan to be immediately despatched to the royal presence. 9. After the presentation of this prince, the necessary money for the outfit of the horse and artillery to be made over by the Persian government to the sirdars of Candahar; Sirdar Mehrdil Khan to be then sent with a thousand horse to the royal camp. This prince being presented, and mutual confidence being established between the shah and the sirdars, no other demand to be made upon the Candaharees by the Persian Government than that of military service. Should Mahomed Shah fail to fulfil any of these several conditions, or depart in any way from the stipulations, I, as minister plenipotentiary of the Russian government, becoming myself responsible, will oblige him in whatever way may be necessary, to act fully up to the terms and conditions of the treaty."

In communicating this remarkable document to the chief authorities Mr. McNeill stated, with great force :—

"The question of Herat seems, therefore, to

be the question of all Afghanistan; and if the place should fall without any attempt having been made to save it, I feel convinced that the moral influence of that event would have a most prejudicial effect on our national reputation in all these countries; for it is no secret to any one that the British government has been desirous to prevent its fall; and that Russia, on the contrary, has been solicitous to see it in the hands of Persia. All Central Asia will regard it as a question between the greater powers, whose views are so publicly spoken of that I did not converse with a villager between Tehran and this place who did not ask me whether the Russians did not favour, and the English oppose, the shah's enterprise against Herat." In the same despatch Mr. McNeill pointed out to Lord Auckland the beneficial effect the advance of a British force in that direction would have, not only upon the shah of Persia, but upon all the rulers of Central Asia.

The English government unfortunately did not act promptly; hence the disasters in Afghanistan that subsequently caused such excitement, and the continued resistance of Persia to our demands. The real nature of the struggle was at length better understood, even by English ministers; and, although they did not meet the emergency with promptness, they eventually decided upon action. Mr. McNeill declared: "I would, therefore, if I could venture to do so, save Herat, which would be saving all Afghanistan;" and on the 16th of May, 1838, this energetic minister obtained an audience of the Persian monarch, and delivered the following memorandum of the demands of the English government:—

"1. That the Persian government shall conclude an equitable arrangement with the government of Herat, and shall cease to weaken and disturb these countries. 2. That the Persian government, according to the stipulations of the general treaty, shall conclude a commercial treaty with Great Britain, and that it shall place the commercial agents of Great Britain on the same footing, with respect to privileges, &c., as the consuls of other powers. 3. That the persons who seized and ill-treated Ali Mahomed Beg, a messenger of the British mission, shall be punished; and that a firman shall be issued such as may prevent the recurrence of so flagrant a violation of the laws and customs of nations. 4. That the Persian government shall publicly abandon the pretension it has advanced to a right to seize and punish the Persian servants of the British mission, without reference to the British minister. 5. That the governor of Bushire, who threatened the safety of the British resident there, shall be removed; that the other persons concerned in that transaction shall be punished; and that measures shall be taken to prevent the recurrence of such proceedings."

The shah of Persia at first professed a willingness to accede to these demands, but the influence of Russia regained the ascendancy, the siege of Herat was resumed, and the remonstrances of the English set at nought. After repeated attempts to bring the monarch of Persia to his senses, Mr. McNeill, on the 7th of June, 1838, quitted the Persian camp, and suspended relations between the two governments. Fully alive to the vital importance of the matter, and of the advantage of striking a blow that should have the effect of awing both the Persians and the Afghans, Mr. McNeill endeavoured to impress upon the government the necessity of saving Herat, which he declared to be the key of Afghanistan. "The country," argued Mr. McNeill, whilst at Meshed, "between the frontiers of Persia and India is far more productive than I had imagined it to be; and there is no impediment, either from the physical features of the country, or from the deficiency of supplies, to the march of a large army from the frontiers of Georgia to Candahar, or, as I believe, to the Indus. Count Simonich, being lame from a wound, drove his carriage from Tehran to Herat, and could drive it to Candahar; and the shah's army has now for nearly seven months subsisted almost exclusively on the supplies of the country immediately around Herat and Ghorian, leaving the still more productive districts of Subzar and Furrah untouched. In short, I can state from personal observation that there is absolutely no impediment to the march of an army to Herat; and that, from all the information I have received, the country between that city and Candahar not only presents no difficulty, but affords remarkable facilities for the passage of armies. There is therefore no security for India in the nature of the country through which an enemy would have to pass to invade it from this side. On the contrary, the whole line is peculiarly favourable for such an enterprise; and I am the more anxious to state this opinion clearly, because it is at variance with my previous belief, and with statements which I may have previously hazarded, relying on more imperfect information. Under such circumstances, it appears to me that it would be a most hazardous policy to allow Persia to act as the pioneer of Russia, and, under protection of the article of the treaty, to break down the main defence of Afghanistan, and thereby make the country untenable to us, at a moment when the concert between Persia and Russia in these operations is avowed. I shall therefore urge Lord Auckland, by every argument I can call to mind, to take a decided course, and to save Herat. . . . It is currently reported and believed here, though I cannot say on what grounds, that there is a secret arrangement between Persia and Russia to exchange Herat for some of the districts beyond the Arras which formerly belonged to Persia. This report was first mentioned to me at Tehran, in March last; but I then paid no attention to it, because I could not see how Russia was to get at Herat; and I still am inclined to regard it as probably unfounded, though Count Simonich certainly threatened Mahomed Ameen, a servant of Yar Mahomed Khan (who was sent with a message from his master to the Persian camp), that, if Herat did not surrender to the shah, he would march a Russian army against it."

Herat defended itself gallantly. The Afghans, under the direction of Lieutenant Pottinger, defeated the Persians in several contests, and thus completely baffled the designs of Persia acting under the inspiration of Russia. Preparations were at length commenced in the north of British India, British troops were dispatched to the island of Karrack in the Persian Gulf, and a naval armament assembled. "The arrival of even the small force," says Mr. McNeill, writing to Lord Palmerston on the 31st of July, 1838, "which has occupied Karrack, has caused a great sensation all over Persia. The intelligence of that event must already have arrived in camp direct from Shiraz, and the loss sustained by the Persian army in the assault, especially the loss of its most efficient and bravest officers, may perhaps prepare the shah to attend to what Colonel Stoddart is instructed to state to him; but I am not sanguine in hoping for this result; the failure of the missions from the Indian government to Cabul and Candahar, and the success of the Russian negotiations with the chiefs on our very frontier, must give the shah a more exalted opinion than even he has hitherto entertained of the superior power of Russia as compared with that of England. He sees an unknown captain of Cossacks, from the banks of the Volga or the Emba, ride up to Cabul without pomp or retinue, and he sees him apparently driving out of Afghanistan the agent of the Governor-general of India, and that agent Captain Burnes, who enjoys a reputation as high and extensive as any officer who could have been employed upon that duty.

"It is now certain that Captain Burnes's departure from Cabul, or at least the determination of Dost Mahomed Khan, which led to his departure, was known in the shah's camp long before I left it—though I did not then credit the reports to that effect which were brought by the emissaries from Candahar; and I therefore cease to wonder at the course pursued by the Persian government in regard to the demands I made upon it, and to the treaty with Herat which it had accepted, and which, on the arrival of intelligence from Candahar, it hastened to reject."

The Shah of Persia was not willing to concede to the terms demanded by the British minister, although afraid to provoke the hostility of England, and he made an attempt at further negotiation. The influence of the Russian agents, however, prevailed, and rendered him refractory. "At this moment," Mr. McNeill stated, on the 3rd of August, 1838, "the united influence of Persia and

Russia would appear to be established in all the Afghan dominions, with the single exception of Herat: and the existence of that influence in those countries, viewed in conjunction with the course which these powers have recently been pursuing, and the measures that have resulted from their joint diplomatic exertions, is so obviously incompatible with the tranquillity of India, and even with its security, that no measures can be more unequivocally measures of self-defence than those which the British government is called upon to adopt for the purpose of counteracting the evils with which India is threatened. Persia has no provocation to complain of. The course pursued by the British government towards this government has been one of uniform friendship and forbearance; and it appears to me that it would be an inefficient, as well as a hazardous and costly line of policy to adopt, were the British government any longer to permit Persia, under the shelter of her treaty with England, to open the way to India for another and far more formidable power."

An intimation was at length conveyed to the Persian monarch, to the effect that the prosecution on his part of the siege of Herat would lead to a declaration of war by Great Britain; and in the autumn of 1838, after some hesitation, all the demands of the British minister were accorded. Upon various pretences the shah sought to gain time, and did not seem actuated by good faith. To Mr. McNeill, however, he made some reparation, and on the 7th of November addressed the following firman to that gentleman:—

"Let it be known to the minister plenipotentiary of the British government that the high in rank Colonel Sheil, secretary (first writer) of the legation, had the honour of being presented to us at Deb Nimuck, and delivered to us your letter, and we have understood its contents. Your excellency wrote that we had preferred the preservation of the friendship with England to the capture of Herat, and that we had counteracted the counsels of designing persons. We offer our thanks to the Lord of the universe that He has preserved our pure nature and our brilliant existence from all violation of treaties and engagements, and from all breach of friendships and alliance, and that He has prevented us from accepting the counsels of the designing. We have not for an instant disregarded the preservation of the terms of the August Treaty, and we have not taken one step which is at variance with friendship. If, as your excellency has represented, the British government desires to renovate the intercourse of friendship and to confirm the alliance, doubtless the difference which has occurred will be adjusted by both parties, and the ancient friendship will be restored to its former condition.

"Let your excellency make known your requests, and consider them about to be accomplished."

The Persian camp broke up on the 9th of September, 1838, the siege of Herat was abandoned, apologies were made to our minister, and a firman was issued to the following effect: "That if a crime should be committed by a servant of the English mission, whether he be a native of Persia or not a native of Persia, which shall be deserving of punishment, his crime shall be investigated and decided upon in the presence of one of the members of the English mission, nor shall any measures be taken for the punishment of the guilty person unless one of the members of the English mission be present."

In the meantime the Persian government did not adhere faithfully to its engagements. With reference to the outrage offered to the British messenger adequate satisfaction was not afforded, nor did Mr. McNeill receive the apologies that had been promised. Moreover, by refusing to evacuate the fort of Ghorian, the shah gave further evidence of his insincerity. Colonel Sheil, secretary of legation, proceeded to the Persian court, and exerted himself strenuously in order to induce the shah to fulfil his engagements.

The conduct pursued by Russia in these transactions became the subject of a correspondence between the courts of London and St. Petersburg. Many of the acts of the Russian agents were disavowed, and, in a conversation with Lord Clanricarde, Count Nesselrode admitted that Great Britain had reason to complain of their conduct. In a despatch dated the 5th of March, 1839, Count Nesselrode stated, with reference to the treaty between Persia and Candahar, "The draft of convention containing these stipulations reached us in the month of April, 1838. Nothing in that act manifested an aggressive or a hostile design. A strictly defensive system was the basis of the stipulations agreed upon on either side. Notwithstanding this, the emperor would not confirm the guarantee which our minister had given to that act. The engagements recorded in it, although purely defensive, were placed beyond the limits which our august master has laid down for his policy. Consequently his majesty ordered Count Simonich to abstain from making himself guarantee to a transaction to which our cabinet thought it right to remain completely a stranger." At that time Russia did not deem it expedient to risk a quarrel with England, so the acts of her agents were not confirmed, though it was well known that they had been dictated from the Russian capital. Captain Vicovich was accordingly recalled from Candahar, but the seeds of mischief that he had sown were not slow to develop themselves.

The proceedings of the army of the Indus, although connected with these events, do not fall within the scope of our narrative; and the same applies to the disasters that soon after occurred in Afghanistan. That Persia had not submitted without reluctance was evident from the obstacles thrown in the way of the re-establishment of cordial relations. Outrages committed against persons attached to the British missions were so frequent, and the general treatment of the English by Persian officials so insulting, that a rupture between the two countries seemed at one time imminent.

In consequence of these petty annoyances, Sir Frederick Maitland, commander-in-chief of the British naval forces in India, on the 25th of March, 1839, landed some men from the *Wellesley* at Bushire. They were fired upon by the Persians, and a serious affray would have followed, had it not been for the firmness of Sir Frederick. On the 29th, Captain Hennell and all connected with the residency embarked on board the *Wellesley*, and were conveyed to Karrack. In April, Captain Hennell received letters from the governor of Bushire, as well as from the cazee and other Persian authorities, in which they all expressed a strong desire to arrange these differences, and to place matters upon the same footing as they had been previous to the misunderstanding. A letter was also sent to Captain Hennell by Mahomed Hassan Khan, an officer of some rank, who had been directed by the regent of Fars to proceed to Bushire for the purpose of adjusting the dispute. In consequence of these advances Captain Hennell repaired to Bushire in the *Wellesley*, in order to endeavour to effect an accommodation. The interview led to no good results, and Captain Hennell returned to Karrack.

Early in 1838 it had been announced that Hoossein Khan was about to undertake a journey to England, as ambassador from the court of Persia, sent by the shah to congratulate Queen Victoria upon her accession to the throne. In a letter from the Foreign

Office, dated March 20, 1838, Lord Palmerston directed the English ministers at Vienna and Paris to inform Hoossein Khan, upon his arrival in either of those capitals, that he would not be received until full reparation had been made for the outrage offered to the messenger of the British mission on his return from Herat to Tehran. Hoossein Khan proceeded first to Constantinople, at which place he applied to Lord Ponsonby to know whether it would be advisable for him to continue his journey. Lord Ponsonby, under the idea that the dispute had been satisfactorily arranged, intimated to Hoossein Khan that he "did not suppose any impediment continued to exist in the way of his visit to England." The British minister at Vienna again applied for instructions; and on the 8th of February, 1839, Lord Palmerston declared that satisfaction had not been given, and, therefore, if Hoossein Khan should persist in continuing his journey to England, he would, on his arrival, receive no mark of respect whatever, but be left wholly unnoticed by the Government, like any other foreigner who might visit England in his private and individual capacity." This determination was communicated to Hoossein Khan upon his arrival at Vienna, in February, 1839. The Persian ambassador, in his interview with the British minister, at once avowed that the chief object of his embassy was to obtain the recal of Mr. McNeill, against whom he had been entrusted with a long list of grievances in the shah's own handwriting.

The Persian version of the affair of the courier was thus explained by Hoossein Khan. "In consequence of certain events, Mr. McNeill had expressed a wish to the shah to be allowed to send a courier, charged with some communication to the ruler of Herat, as far as Meshed, where he was to have been met by a courier from Kamran to whom he was to deliver the letters of which he was the bearer. Permission to this effect was granted by the shah and the courier set out on his journey, having, however, received from Mr. McNeill secret instructions not to stop at Meshed, but to proceed straight to Herat, and return himself with the answer. This is asserted to have taken place without the knowledge of the shah.

Mr. McNeill's courier succeeded in reaching Herat in safety, and was on his way back to Meshed, accompanied by a servant of Kamran's, when one evening, after dusk, they encountered the outposts of a division of the Persian army, commanded, I think, Hoossein Khan said, by a Polish officer, and having received the customary challenge, instead of answering it, they both galloped off, and were pursued and fired at by some Persian cavalry despatched after them. However, through the superiority of their horses, they succeeded in escaping, but on the following day again presented themselves under the disguise of horse-dealers, and offered their horses for sale to the commander of the division. He not wishing to purchase more than one, but desirous not to lose an opportunity of obtaining valuable animals, detained the two individuals until he had communicated with Hajee Khan, by whom they were sent for to show their horses. On their way to his tent, Mr. McNeill's courier was accidentally recognised by some one, who immediately announced the fact, and this led to an inquiry how he came there, and what was his errand; in the course of which it came out that the other man was in the service of Kamran, and his presence in the Persian camp having naturally inspired some distrust as to his intentions, he narrowly escaped being put to death on the spot as a spy. Mr. McNeill's courier was examined and his despatches taken from him, together with some letters which were found concealed in the soles of his boots; but when it was satisfactorily explained that he was actually employed on the service of Her Majesty's minister, they were returned to him unopened, and he was admonished to continue his journey."

In a despatch to Mr. Milbanke, dated March 8, 1839, Lord Palmerston declared the Persian version of the affair of the courier to be at variance with the official reports of the transaction received by the English authorities, the correctness of which they did not for one moment doubt, and refused to recal Mr. McNeill.

Hoossein Khan had in the meantime endeavoured to interest Prince Metternich in his behalf. To that distinguished statesman the

Persian ambassador described the political attitude of the shah:—"The shah is sovereign of his country, and as such he desires to be independent. There are two great powers with whom Persia is in more or less direct contact,—Russia, and the English power in India. The first has more military means than the second: on the other hand, England has more money than Russia. The two powers can thus do Persia good and evil; and in order above all to avoid the evil, the shah is desirous of keeping himself, with respect to them, within the relations of good friendship and free from all contestation. If, on the contrary, he finds himself threatened on one side, he will betake himself to the other in search of the support which he shall stand in need of. That is not what he desires, but to what he may be driven, for he is not more the friend of one than of the other of those powers: he desires to be with them on a footing of equal friendship. What he cherishes above all is his independence, and the maintenance of good relations with foreign powers."

Hoossein Khan persisted in asserting that

Mr. McNeill was the real cause of the estrangement between England and Persia; and assured Prince Metternich that he should continue his journey in spite of every obstacle. Prince Metternich undertook to transmit to the English government a memorandum drawn up by the Persian ambassador himself; and Hoossein Khan at length consented to wait at Vienna until a reply had been received. In forwarding this document to M. de Hummelauer, for presentation to the English authorities, Prince Metternich remarked—"Hoossein Khan gives me the idea of a man gifted with a large measure of understanding and an accurate knowledge of the state of affairs in Europe. He expresses himself very well, and he could scarcely be better than he is if he had passed many years in the midst of Christian civilization. I have taken care to give you exactly the very words he addressed to me, and which are remarkable for a degree of precision which is scarcely Eastern."

The memorandum was returned by Lord Palmerston, with the remark that "it is, from beginning to end, an entire perversion and misrepresentation of the facts to which it relates."

After various other efforts, Hoossein Khan proceeded to Paris, in April ; but, failing to make any impression upon Earl Granville, the British minister at that court, he obtained a passport from the French authorities, to enable him to visit England as a private individual. Furnished with this, Hoossein Khan reached London in June, 1839, and, on the 19th, was admitted to a conference with Lord Palmerston, in Stanhope Street. On this occasion, the English minister reiterated his refusal to present the letter from the shah to the Queen of England, brought by the Persian ambassador, until the demands of England had been satisfied. In vain Hoossein Khan endeavoured to shake Lord Palmerston's determination. On the 11th of July, a memorandum was presented to the Persian ambassador in which those demands were thus set forth :—

"First, That a written apology shall be made to the British government for what happened with regard to the British messenger; that apology should not be accompanied by any objectionable matter, and might be made either by the prime minister, the hajee, or, if the shah prefers it, by a letter from the shah to the queen. Secondly, That a firman shall be published in Persia, and a copy of it be communicated to the British government, assuring protection to all persons, whether British, Persian, or others, who may be employed in the service of the British mission. This firman to be in conformity with what was stated in Sir John McNeill's memorandum given to the shah on the 4th of June, 1838. Thirdly, That Ghorian and the other places in Afghanistan which have been occupied by the Persian garrisons, shall be evacuated by the Persian troops, and be restored to the Afghans. Fourthly, That a written apology shall be made by the Persian government for the attempt made by Major General Semino to seize the house at Tehran, which the shah had placed at the disposal of Major Todd. Fifthly, That all persons concerned in the outrage committed on the person and property of the broker of the British residency at Bushire, in the month of November last, shall be punished. Sixthly, That the governor of Bushire, who was guilty of the affront lately offered to Sir F. Maitland, the British admiral, shall be removed from his command, and that the reason of his removal shall be publicly made known by the Persian government. Seventhly, That the claims of Sir Henry Bethune on account of the iron-works in Karadagh shall be liquidated. Eighthly, That the sums due to the British officers shall be paid. Ninthly, That the signature of a commercial treaty between Great Britain and Persia shall accompany the re-establishment of diplomatic relations between the two states.

"Viscount Palmerston has further to state, that Colonel Sheil, Her Majesty's *chargé d'affaires*, has been ordered to remain at Erzeroom, in order to be at hand to receive any communication which the Persian government may have to make to that of Great Britain; and, in conclusion, Viscount Palmerston begs to remark that Hoossein Khan, in his letter to Viscount Palmerston, gives the Queen the inferior title of *Malikeh* instead of the title of *Padshah*, which properly belongs to her Majesty, and which the British government expect to be used in any official communication which they may receive from the government of Persia."

Another conference between Lord Palmerston and Hoossein Khan was held at Stanhope Street, on the 13th of July: at which, in spite of a long discussion, no satisfactory conclusion was arrived at.

After various negotiations, Meerza Massood, the Persian minister of foreign affairs, in a communication dated the 20th of September, 1839, expressed the willingness of the shah to comply with the demands of the English government. Unnecessary delays were, however, thrown in the way of the execution of some of these pledges, and a long interval elapsed before friendly relations were completely re-established. The treaty of commerce was not concluded until the 28th of October, 1841. It was signed at Tehran, and contained the following articles:—

"Article I. The merchants of the two mighty states are reciprocally permitted and allowed to carry into each other's territories their goods and manufactures of every description, and to sell or exchange them in any part of their respective countries; and on the goods which they import or export, custom duties shall be levied, that is to say, on entering the country the same amount of custom duties shall be levied, once for all, that is levied on merchandise imported by the merchants of the most favoured European nations; and at the time of going out of the country, the same amount of custom duties which is levied on the merchandise of merchants of the most favoured European nations shall be levied from the merchants subjects of the high contracting parties; and except this, no claim shall be made upon the merchants of the two states in each other's dominions on any pretext or under any denomination; and the merchants or persons connected with or dependent upon the high contracting parties in each other's dominions, mutually, shall receive the same aid and support, and the same respect, which are received by the subjects of the most favoured nations.

"Article II. As it is necessary, for the

purpose of attending to the affairs of the merchants of the two parties respectively, that from both governments commercial agents should be appointed to reside in stated places: it is therefore arranged that two commercial agents on the part of the British government shall reside, one in the capital, and one in Tabreez, and in those places only, and on this condition, that he who shall reside at Tabreez, and he alone, shall be honoured with the privileges of consul-general; and as for a series of years a resident of the British government has resided at Bushire, the Persian government grants permission that the said resident shall reside there as heretofore. And, in like manner, two commercial agents shall reside on the part of the Persian government, one in the capital, London, and one in the port of Bombay, and shall enjoy the same rank and privileges which the commercial agents of the British government shall enjoy in Persia."

Thus, after protracted negotiations, these various matters were adjusted, and harmony between the two governments restored.

In the foregoing narrative our object has

been to give the reader an accurate idea of the progress of events, without pausing to indulge in criticism, or to propound opinions. The importance of Herat, and the necessity of keeping it free from Russian influences, cannot admit of the slightest doubt. One of the latest authorities, Mr. Kaye, in his History of the war in Afghanistan, thus describes this important place:—"Situated at that point of the great range of mountains bounding the whole of our northern frontier, even to Assam, which alone presents facilities to the transport of a train of heavy artillery, Herat has, with no exaggeration, been described as the gate of India. Within the limits of the Heratee territory, all the great roads leading on India converge. At other points, between Herat and Cabul, a body of troops unencumbered with guns, or having only a light field artillery, might make good its passage, if not actively opposed, across the stupendous mountain ranges of the Hindoo-Kaash; but it is only by the Herat route that a really formidable, well-equipped army could make its way upon the Indian frontier from the regions on the north-west. Both the nature and the resources of the country are such as to favour the success of the invader. All the materials necessary for the organization of a great army, and the formation of his depôts, are to be found in the neighbourhood of Herat. Its mines supply lead, iron, and sulphur; the surface in almost every direction is laden with saltpetre; the willow and the poplar trees, which furnish the best charcoal, flourish in all parts; whilst from the population might, at any time, be drawn hardy and docile soldiers to recruit the ranks of an invading army. Upon the possession of such a country would depend, in no small measure, the success of operations undertaken for the invasion, or the defence of Hindostan."

The connection between these events and our subsequent disasters in Afghanistan, the intrigues of Russia, and the nature of the various influences at work, are stated with great force and clearness by a writer in the "Quarterly Review," for June, 1839. His lucid statement will afford the reader a just conception of the plot in progress, which was only frustrated by the obstinate resistance of

Herat, and the foresight and energy of the British agents in the East. This writer says:—

"An active intercourse was carried on between the chiefs of Cabul and Candahar and the court of the shah, in which the Russian minister, in concert with the Persian government, played an important part. The increasing power of the Seiks; the success which had hitherto attended their able and warlike sovereign, Runjeet Sing, in all his contests with the Afghans; and especially the establishment of his authority over Peshawur, and some other places on the western bank of the Indus, which were inhabited by a Mahomedan population, had excited at once the fears and the religious enthusiasm of the chiefs of Cabul and Candahar. At the same time, the connection which was supposed to exist between the English and the exiled sovereigns of Afghanistan, who had found an asylum in the British territories,—the opinion which prevailed, that the government had favoured the unsuccessful attempt which Shah Shoojah had made on a former occasion to recover his kingdom,—the intimate relations of friendship which were known to have subsisted for many years between the British government in India and the court of Lahore,—and, more than all, the total neglect with which the British government had hitherto treated these Afghan chiefs,—had led them to regard England with feelings of jealousy rather than of attachment; and had induced them to seek, in alliances with Persia and Russia, protection against the dangers with which they believed themselves to be threatened from the East. The chief of Cabul sent accredited agents almost simultaneously to the courts of Tehran and St. Petersburg, soliciting from both assistance against the Seiks. The chiefs of Candahar also sent agents into Persia; but as the greatest danger which they apprehended was from the power of Kamran, prince of Herat, their chief object was to concert with Persia a combined attack for the destruction of that power.

"But although the chiefs of Cabul and Candahar thus found in the nature of their external relations a reason for seeking to connect themselves more intimately with Persia, there were also circumstances in the internal condition of the countries they governed, and in their own positions in respect to the Afghan nations, which led them to desire the countenance and support of the shah. They were usurpers—they had driven from the throne the descendant of Ahmed Shah—the representative of the Afghan monarchy and the chief of the tribe Suddozye. They knew that the Afghan people, however they might have been misled by intrigues, irritated by ill-treatment, and excited by ambition or by personal enmities, to aid in expelling princes of the royal family, still regarded with feelings of attachment or of reverence every member of that house, and they therefore distrusted the feelings of the Afghan people towards themselves. There were, both at Cabul and at Candahar, Persian tribes which had been settled there by Nâdir—in effect, colonies of hereditary soldiers, who were powerful by their union, by their military skill and reputation, and by their superior acuteness and intelligence. The chiefs of Cabul and Candahar, dreading the influence of the Suddozyes, and doubting the attachment of the majority of the Afghans, early connected themselves with these Persian, or, as they are usually called, Kizzilbash tribes. But the Kizzilbashes had retained their language, their religion, and their attachment to their father-land. They were still Persians and Sheeahs in the midst of an Afghan and Sooney population. By their connection with the Barikzye chiefs they had become a dominant people, both at Cabul and at Candahar, and they shared with these chiefs the apprehension that the affection of the Afghans for the Suddozyes might one day restore that exiled family to the kingdom, and give the Afghan people, properly so called, the ascendancy in their own country, which they had lost during the usurpation of the present rulers of Cabul and Candahar. They therefore naturally turned to Persia, to their native country, for the support which was not only to defend them from foreign aggression and from internal revolution, but to confirm them in their dominant position in the country in which they were still regarded as strangers. They felt that, if the chiefs whom they served could be made to lean on Persia for support,

Persian influence must from that moment be firmly established; and that they, being the actual representatives of their nation in Afghanistan, must then become more necessary to their chiefs, and the favoured instruments of the shah. They, therefore, exerted all their influence, which was great, in favour of the connection with Persia; and, as there were apprehensions in the minds of their rulers that Persia alone might not be strong enough to defend them, they advocated the advantages of an alliance with Russia also—for they were told by the agents of both these governments that Persia and Russia were one.

"The shah of Persia saw in this state of things at Cabul and Candahar a prospect of establishing his own supremacy over all Afghanistan, and the means of promoting the immediate success of the favourite object of his ambition—the subjugation of Herat. The Russian agents, on the other hand, thought they had discovered in these combinations the means of establishing Russian influence in all these countries, and of striking a blow at England. In Persia, the great impediment to the success of Russia's views had hitherto been the perfect community of interests between Great Britain and Persia, which had united them, not more by formal engagements than by a sense of common danger, in an intimate alliance for their mutual defence; and, so long as the late shah lived, this sentiment had had its full weight in the councils of Persia. But the young shah, after mounting the throne, had removed all experienced or wise councillors from around him, and had placed the affairs of his empire entirely in the hands of persons who shared in the love of conquest by which he was himself actuated. To enable him to prosecute these schemes, it was necessary that he should so cultivate intimate relations with Russia as to relieve him from all apprehension that, while he was engaged on distant expeditions, Russia would profit by his absence to disturb or dismember his kingdom; and he was taught to believe that, if he could insure the support of Russia, England would not venture to oppose him. But he felt that the first and most essential step towards gaining the entire confidence of

Russia, was to detach himself from England. The Russian agents, therefore, perceived that, to induce him to prosecute his projects of military conquest and of aggrandizement in Afghanistan was the most effectual mode of leading him to transfer his confidence from England to Russia, and that it must ultimately lead to an opposition of interests between England and Persia, and a community of objects between Persia and Russia, which could not fail to further their own schemes. Though, in the early part of these transactions, they professed to desire only the success of the shah's enterprises and the advancement of his interests, they gradually unfolded to him their own views and intentions, which exhibited a community of interests between Persia and Russia hitherto undiscovered, and a common opposition to England, which Persia had never before contemplated. In furtherance of the concerted projects of these parties, an envoy was sent by the shah to Candahar and Cabul, charged with presents and communications, not only from his Persian majesty, but also from the Russian minister at the Persian court."

CHAPTER IV.

Causes that produced the Rupture between England and Persia in 1856.

Although friendly relations had been re-established between the governments of England and Persia, and all causes of dispute apparently removed, the irritating influence of Russia gradually produced another estrangement. The shah, by following the advice of the Russian agents, was precipitated upon a factious course of opposition to England, both as regarded the treatment of persons belonging to the British missions, and her attitude with respect to Herat. Upon the death of Yar Mahomed Khan, in 1851, Lieutenant-Colonel Sheil, at that time British minister at the Persian court, obtained information that an expedition against Herat was to be organized under the command of Sultan Moorad Meerza, the governor of Khorassan. Against this proceeding, Colonel Sheil remonstrated forcibly. On the 21st of July, 1851, the British minister had an interview with Ameer Nizam, at which, to use his own words, "I informed him that the views of the British government with respect to Herat, were unchanged; that it would allow of no interference with that city; and that any demonstration of Sultan Moorad Meerza in that direction would be followed by evil consequences; and that it appeared to me it was for the interest of the Persian government to give me assurances of the course it intended to adopt, in order that I might communicate these assurances, without delay, both to her Majesty's government and the government of India." The Persian minister denied that any movement against Herat was intended; declaring that the expedition was designed solely for the purpose of coercing the Tejjen Toorkomans.

Rumours were, however, in circulation to the effect, that the Governor of Khorassan intended to afford military aid to Shahzadeh Mahomed Youssuf Meerza, a member of a previous dynasty in Herat. This chieftain, it was said, contemplated an attempt to regain the sovereignty, and thus set aside Syed Mahomed Khan, the son of the deceased Yar Mahomed Khan, and his legitimate successor. During the autumn of 1851, the affairs of Herat fell into greater confusion, and Syed Mahomed Khan sent an agent to the shah's camp, to solicit assistance in maintaining his authority. The result of his mission is thus described by Mr. Ronald Thomson:—"Syed Mahomed Khan's messenger quitted the camp some days ago, on his return to Herat. A firman from the shah, and a letter from the ameer, have been transmitted, through this person, in answer to Syed Mahomed Khan's application for assistance to enable him to extricate himself from the danger threatened by the advance of Kohendil Khan, and by the discord and disputes which had arisen among the people of Herat. The shah, it appears, in his firman, has confined himself to expressions of friendship and goodwill to Syed Mahomed Khan, giving him vague promises of assistance, without specifying in what manner, or to what extent, the support of the Persian government will be afforded to him. He calls upon the chief people of Herat to submit to Syed Mahomed Khan's authority, and urges them to support his authority, threatening to punish those who offer him any opposition. The answer which the ameer has returned to his application for support, is said to convey a refusal, at present, to comply with his request; but, at the same time, a prospect of receiving at a future time the assistance which he desires, is held out to him. The ameer has, I am told, given Syed Mahomed Khan to understand, that by issuing coin in the shah's name, and by preparing a paper to be sealed by the chief people of Herat, declaring themselves subject to Persia, the Persian ministers may be induced to extend to him the aid which he has solicited. The messenger is also the bearer of a dress of honour, and a sword with jewelled scabbard, which have been conferred on Syed Mahomed Khan by the shah."

Towards the end of September it was announced in the *Tehran Gazette* that an expedition, consisting of two thousand infantry and six thousand cavalry, was about to proceed to Khorassan, whereupon Colonel Sheil again warned Ameer Nizam that the augmentation of troops in that province, without apparent necessity, would excite suspicion, and probably lead to precautionary measures on the part of the governor-general of India. The Persian minister declared that the alarm was unfounded, and that the only contingency under which Persia would desire to despatch a force to Herat would be the approach of Dost Mahomed Khan or Kohendil Khan to subvert the authority of Syed Mahomed Khan, in which case troops would be at once despatched.

In spite of these denials, intrigues were carried on. In November, Meerza Boozoorg Khan, the agent of Syed Mahomed Khan, returned from Persia to Herat, accompanied by a Persian agent of higher rank than usual, bearing presents of considerable value to the ruler of Herat, from whom he undertook to obtain an acknowledgment of the supremacy of Persia over Herat, by striking coin and by reading the "Kootbeh," or Friday prayer, in the shah's name, which form in the East an indisputable recognition of sovereignty. In the *Tehran Gazette*, Syed Mahomed Khan was styled "governor of Herat," and his presents to the shah were termed "offerings." An agent arrived from Candahar to obtain the consent of the Persian government to an expedition against Herat, and Kohendil Khan accompanied the proposal by a threat. In January, 1852, it was reported that Kohendil Khan had despatched a force from Candahar, under the command of one of his nephews, and that the prince of Khorassan had publicly announced his intention of marching to Herat. Colonel Sheil again remonstrated forcibly with Sadr Azim, the prime minister of Persia, upon these events, and the latter repeated a demand he had before made, that "England should undertake to preserve Herat from the chiefs of Cabul and Candahar, and that then Persia would not interfere; otherwise, that Great Britain should agree to the despatch of a moderate Persian force, with an engagement that it should return in a specific time."

From what passed at the interview, Colonel Sheil was led to believe that the Persians would not advance towards Herat unless the Candahar army approached in another direction.

These hopes, however, proved fallacious. The Persian government soon after despatched a force to Herat, while Syed Mahomed Khan expelled his uncle, Dost Mahomed Khan, from the fort of Ghorian, and sent a body of troops against the Candahar army at Ferrah. In a correspondence with the English minister in January, 1852, Sadr Azim asserted that "the Persian ministers consider Herat, not Afghanistan, to be a portion of the province of Khorassan, and the protection of Herat and the people of Herat to be their duty." He declared further, that "the Persian troops will, with the knowledge of the British ministers, proceed to Herat, in order to secure the tranquillity of Khorassan and the Persian frontiers, and to establish regularity in the affairs of Herat, so that it may remain in its former condition, and having appointed a governor from among the people of Herat, so that the affairs of that place may be put in order, will then return without delay, and without taking possession of it."

Colonel Sheil endeavoured to induce the Persian government to abandon this design, but his remonstrances proved of little avail. In reply to some remarks contained in a communication from the shah, the purport of which was that it affected his dignity not to listen to the supplications of Syed Mahomed Khan, and to refuse to send a body of troops to his assistance, Colonel Sheil wrote: "This is incomprehensible. Let us examine who Syed Mahomed Khan is, and what claim he has to impose this obligation on the sovereign of Persia. He is a man of profound incapacity. He is the son of Yar Mahomed Khan, the slave-dealer and man-stealer,—the traitor, usurper,—the murderer of his sovereign. Is such a person, or are his interests, to be placed in competition with the long-tried friendship of Great Britain? Let him rule if he can, but let not Persia run the risk of coldness with an old ally for so worthless a person."

Warning and remonstrance were alike disregarded, and, in the spring of 1852, the Persian expedition advanced upon Herat. At an interview with Colonel Sheil, on the 14th of March, the shah made four proposals, to none of which the English minister could assent. In his despatches to the home authorities, Colonel Sheil pointed out that indifference or supineness on their part would lead to the permanent annexation of Herat by Persia. The importance of the stake at issue was clearly understood by this minister. Writing on the 4th of May, he said: "The change which has taken place in the British dominions in India, and the advance of the frontier, have, it may be averred, diminished or destroyed the importance of Herat, and rendered its possession a question of indifference. It can scarcely admit of doubt that the annexation of the Punjab and Scinde, and the occupation of the line of the Indus, have immensely increased the strength and power of the British government to repel invasion or aggression. But I think it ought not to be forgotten that the antagonist parties have at the same time approximated, and that the facilities and means of demonstration and aggression have increased. A few years ago England was on the Sutlej, and Russia on the Arras, 1,400 miles from Herat, with the unfruitful Georgian Provinces and the Caucasus behind her. Now Russia is at Asterabad, with the open sea and the Volga in the rear."

Not only was Herat invaded and the city occupied by Persian troops, but several Afghan khans were seized and despatched into Persia. The duplicity practised at this period by the Persian government was altogether disgraceful. Sheffee Khan, their *chargé d'affaires* at the English court, declared officially to Lord Malmesbury that a Persian garrison was not to be left at Herat; yet, at the very time that he was making this declaration, the shah had given orders for its annexation to Persia, and the language of the Persian *chargé d'affaires* was disavowed by the Persian prime minister Sadr Azim, in a conversation with Colonel Sheil in August. In consequence of the discrepancies between these statements, the insincerity of the Persian authorities, and their utter disregard of truth, Lord Malmesbury, on the 27th of October, intimated to Sheffee Khan that he could no longer hold political intercourse either with him or with any other representative of the Persian government in London.

Negotiations were carried on, but the Persian government persisted in annexing Herat; and in October a firman was issued, appointing Syed Mahomed Khan governor of Herat and its dependencies. In announcing this fact to the British government, Colonel Sheil declared: — "Letters from Meshed mention orders having been issued by Syed Mahomed Khan, the ruler of Herat, that henceforward money is to be coined in that principality in the name of the shah; the imprisonment, fining, torture, and execution, by the same person, of various Afghan chiefs, believed to be opposed to the establishment of Persian supremacy; the demand for Persian troops to act in conjunction with those of Herat against Ferrah; the influence acquired by Sam Khan, late Persian political agent in Herat, among the Afghan tribes close to the Candahar frontier; the open assumption of actual sovereignty by Persia, in the despatch of agents by the prince governor of Khorassan to bring to Meshed Afghan chiefs imprisoned in Herat by

Syed Mahomed Khan; and the complete subjection displayed by the latter person to the will of the Persian government."

Failing in his attempts to make any impression upon the Persian government, and disgusted at the levity and insincerity displayed by all, from the shah to the meanest official, Colonel Sheil, in January, 1853, counselled decisive measures, such as the withdrawal of the British mission, and the occupation of the island of Kharg, or Karrack. "This small island," says Colonel Sheil, "is near the head of the Persian Gulf, about thirty miles from Bushire. In the unhealthy climate of that sea, it is the most salubrious spot. It has a good harbour and contains excellent water, from which Bushire is chiefly supplied. From its position, it commands the mouths of the Shat-ool-Arab, or joint stream of the Euphrates and Tigris, and in English hands is fitted to exercise control over the coast on both sides of the gulf. I make no comment on the advantages which commerce would, hereafter, derive from such a position. I do not mean to convey the opinion that Karrack is an equivalent for the transfer of Herat to Persia. That island is certainly, however, not without value."

Colonel Sheil continued to oppose energetically, any movement of Persian troops towards Herat, and in the course of these discussions, an uncourteous expression was applied to Lord Malmesbury; of which, however, an explanation was afterwards attempted. The English government remained firm; and after various negotiations, the shah conceded the principal points in dispute, and on the 25th of January, 1853, the following engagement, respecting Herat, was signed. Two translations of this document are given in the Parliamentary papers, of which we select the second, made by Mr. Ronald F. Thomson, under the direction of the Hon. C. A. Murray:—

"The Persian government engages not to send troops, on any account, to the territory of Herat, excepting when troops from without attack that place; that is to say, troops from the direction of Cabul, or from Candahar, or from other foreign territory; and in case of troops being despatched under such circumstances, the Persian government binds itself that they shall not enter the city of Herat; and that immediately on the retreat of the foreign troops to their own country, the Persian force shall forthwith return to the Persian soil without delay. The Persian government also engages to abstain from all interferenee whatsoever in the internal affairs of Herat, likewise in (regard to) occupation, or taking possession, or assuming the sovereignty or government, except that the same amount of interference which took place between the two in the time of the late Zuheer-ud-Dowleh, Yar Mahomed Khan, is to exist as formerly. The Persian government, therefore, engages to address a letter to Syed Mahomed Khan, acquainting him with these conditions, and to forward it to him (by a person), accompanied by some one belonging to the English mission who may be in Meshed.

"The Persian government also engages to relinquish all claim or pretension to the coinage of money, and to the 'khootbeh,' or to any other mark whatever of subjection or of allegiance on the part of the people of Herat to

Persia. But if, as in the time of the late Kamran, and in that of the late Yar Mahomed Khan, they should, of their own accord, send an offering in money, and strike it in the shah's name, Persia will receive it without making any objection. This condition will also be immediately communicated to Syed Mahomed Khan. They also engage to recall Abbass Koolee Khan, Peeseean, after four months from the date of his arrival, so that he may not reside there permanently; and hereafter no permanent agent will be placed in Herat, but intercourse will be maintained as in the time of Yar Mahomed Khan. Neither will they maintain a permanent agent on the part of Herat in Tehran. There will be the same relations and privileges which existed in Kamran's time, and in that of the late Yar Mahomed Khan. For instance, if at any time it should be necessary, for the punishment of the Toorkomans, or in case of disturbance or rebellion in the shah's dominions, that the Persian government should receive assistance from the Heratees, similar to that afforded by the late Yar Mahomed Khan, they may, as formerly, render assistance of their own accord and free will, but not of a permanent nature.

"The Persian government further engages, unconditionally and without exception, to release and set free all the chiefs of Herat who are in Meshed, or in Tehran, or in any other part of Persia, and not to receive any offenders, prisoners, or suspected persons whatsoever, from Syed Mahomed Khan, with the exception of such persons as, having been banished by Syed Mahomed Khan from Herat, may come here and themselves desire to remain, or to enter the service. These will be treated with kindness and favour as formerly. Distinct orders will be issued immediately to the Prince Governor of Khorassan to carry out these engagements.

"The above six engagements, on the part of the Persian government, are to be observed, and to have effect; and the Persian ministers, notwithstanding the rights which they possess in Herat, solely out of friendship and to satisfy the English government, have entered into these engagements with the English government, so long as there is no interference whatsoever on its part in the internal affairs of Herat and its dependencies; otherwise, these engagements will be null and void, and as if they never had existed or been written. And if any foreign (state), either Afghan or other, should desire to interfere with or encroach upon the territory of Herat or its dependencies, and the Persian ministers should make the request, the British government are not to be remiss in restraining them, and in giving their friendly advice, so that Herat may remain in its own state of independence."

A dispatch in virtue of this convention, was addressed by Sadr Azim to Syed Mahomed Khan, ruler of Herat, together with a firman from the shah, and these, with another communication from the British minister, were, by the latter, enclosed to Syed Mahomed Khan.

The Persian government were not, however, sincere in their acceptance of these conditions, as is evident from the manner in which they continued to throw obstacles in the way of the settlement to which they had agreed. They objected to the person chosen by Colonel Sheil to accompany the Persian messenger to Herat.

This man, Sultan Khan, happened to be a native of Candahar; on which account, Meerza Saeed Khan, the Persian minister of foreign affairs, contended, that he would "engage in other matters unconnected with the affair in question;" and actually threatened not to adhere to their engagements unless the appointment was cancelled. Colonel Sheil refused to yield to their dictation; and ultimately the Persian ministers, with evident reluctance, gave way.

"The Persian character," says Malcolm, "throughout all its shades has one predominant feature—an overweening vanity distinguishes the whole nation." The observation is just; and this failing in the subjects of a weak state is certain to produce repeated complications. New difficulties soon arose, of which the first appears to have had reference to the appointment of Meerza Hashem Khan. On the 15th of June, 1854, Mr. W. T. Thomson wrote to Lord Clarendon, stating that he had named this person first Persian secretary to the British mission at Tehran. "He is," says Mr. Thomson, "about thirty years of age, and belongs to one of the chief branches of the tribe of Nooree, but not that of which Sadr Azim is the representative. His father, the late Meerza Mahomed Raheem Khan was, during the last reign, on different occasions, governor of the districts of Mishkeen, of Sirab, and of Meeaneh; and, having commenced his service in the household of the present shah while heir-apparent, he has a most extensive circle of acquaintance among the people of the court. The late Ameer Nizam was his patron, and, a few days before he was seized and exiled to Cashan, intended to have given him a post in the civil service; but, since that minister's fall, he has received no countenance from his successor. His character, in as far as I have been able to ascertain, is most respectable, and he is connected by marriage with the royal family."

Of this appointment Lord Clarendon approved, but the Persian government declined to receive Meerza Hashem Khan in the capacity to which he had been nominated, on the plea that, having been in the service of the shah, and not having received a formal discharge, he was not competent to enter any other service. This was merely a pretext; but Mr. Thomson named Meerza Fezloollah in his stead, and intimated that when Meerza Hashem Khan received a formal discharge from the Persian government he would be appointed to the post of British agent at Shiraz. The Hon. C. A. Murray wrote to Lord Clarendon on the 22nd of June, 1855, requesting him to sanction the appointment, and this the English minister of foreign affairs did in a despatch, dated August 1.*

The enmity of the Persian government against Meerza Hashem was not to be easily overcome; and, on the 6th of November, 1855, Sadr Azim informed Mr. Murray that if he attempted to set out for Shiraz the Persian government would cause him to be seized and detained.

The next step in the transaction was the

* A writer in the *Quarterly Review* (April, 1857) states that this appointment was made by Mr. Murray. The evidence of the blue book is, however, conclusive upon this point. The appointment was recommended by Mr. Thomson, received the approval of Mr. Murray, and was afterwards confirmed by Lord Clarendon.

seizure and detention of the wife of Meerza Hashem by order of the Persian government. Mr. Murray at once demanded this lady's release; and the Persian prime minister replied by refusing to enter on a discussion regarding such a delicate subject as ladies connected with the royal harem. On Saturday, the 17th of November, Mr. Murray gave official notice that, if Meerza Hashem Khan's wife was not liberated and restored to her husband by twelve at noon on the ensuing Monday, the flag of the British mission would be hauled down and friendly relations broken off. Negotiations were carried on; the Ottoman *chargé d'affaires* and the French minister endeavoured to mediate; but the insincerity displayed by the Persian authorities in all their proceedings prevented an accommodation, and on the 20th of November, Mr. Murray struck his flag.

To render matters worse, Sadr Azim, the Persian prime minister, on two several occasions, stated to two European gentlemen, both holding official situations at Tehran, that the reason why Mr. Thomson first took Meerza

Hashem Khan into the British mission and retained him under protection was, because he had an intrigue with Meerza Hashem's wife; and he afterwards made the same statement with reference to Mr. Murray, as his reason for continuing the protection and employment of the meerza, and spread these reports through the shah's palace. On the 19th of November, allusions and insinuations of the kind were made in a despatch sent by Sadr Azim to Mr. Murray; and these matters materially increased the difficulties of the case.

Relations between the two states having been suspended, an angry correspondence was for some time carried on between the Persian government and Mr. Murray; but the necessary concessions were refused; and on the 5th of December, 1855, he withdrew his mission from Tehran. The satisfaction which the British minister demanded as the condition of resuming diplomatic relations and re-hoisting his flag, was:—

"1. Meerza Hashem Khan's wife to be released and restored to her husband, and he himself to be recognized as in the employment of the mission. 2. The Sadr Azim to visit me at the mission to apologise for the offensive despatch, and to withdraw it; as also to retract whatever charges he had made, either here or in writing to foreign governments, calumniating myself and the mission in respect to improper relations with Meerza Hashem Khan's wife. 3. One of three high officers whom I named to call at the mission on the part of the shah to apologise for that most offensive sentence contained in the royal autograph letter, and to withdraw the letter itself. 4. As the Moollahs have been induced by the Sadr Azim to affix the seals of many of them to a document containing similar charges against myself and the mission, directly tending to bring the mission and her majesty's government into contempt and odium among the Persian people, the chiefs of that body to call at the mission to express to me their utter disbelief of the above-named calumnies, and to give me their assurance that they would contradict them wheresoever they might hear them repeated."

The scene then changed to Constantinople, at which city the Persian *chargé d'affaires* sought an interview with Lord Stratford de Redcliffe, which he obtained on the 2nd of January, 1856. To Lord Stratford the Persian diplomatist deplored the rupture, and delivered to him a communication from the Persian prime minister, complaining of Mr. Murray's conduct, and professing to give the Persian version of the affair. Great complaints were also made, both of Mr. Thomson and Mr. Stevens; in fact, all the representatives of England in Persia came in for a share of censure. On the 22nd of November, 1855, the shah himself, in an autograph note to the Persian minister for foreign affairs, wrote, with reference to the last-mentioned gentleman: "With regard to what he* has written, that he will leave a consul here—if by consul he means Mr. Stevens, whose proceedings and mischief-making, while living in Tabreez, would fill ten books, and whose proceedings here are just what you now

* The Hon. C. A. Murray.

see—when Mr. Murray, as minister plenipotentiary, has become the cause of coolness and misunderstanding in this way between the two governments—what are we to expect, and what confidence can we have in a person like Mr. Stevens, notorious for his mischief-making? If the British minister goes, let him take with him Mr. Stevens; let him place some one else in his place. Send a copy of this autograph in answer to the minister's letter, and prepare the details of his conduct for the information of the British ministers, together with the real truth of the question. If the British minister desires the humiliation of this government, of course we, so long as we have the power, will not submit to any indignity."

In the Persian minister's memorandum, and in a paper drawn up by the Persian ministers for publication in Europe, the conduct of British ministers in Persia formed the subject of complaint. Mr. McNeill, Colonel Sheil, Colonel Farrant, Mr. Thomson, and Mr. Murray, were all severely censured, In the latter document the charge against Mr. Murray, with respect to Meerza Hashem Khan's wife, was repeated, and his proceedings on his arrival in Persia were denominated "spicy."

In the Persian vindication, by the Persian ministers, the affair of Meerza Hashem Khan and his wife is thus stated:—

"Meerza Hashem Khan, from what has become known, was first of all employed as a page in the late shah's harem, and afterwards accompanied Nassir-oon-deen Shah, then heir-apparent, when he went to Azerbijan. When the shah returned from that province to Tehran, and ascended the throne, Meerza Hashem Khan was appointed, on a salary of two hundred tomauns a year, to be a Gholam Pish-khidmet to his majesty.[a] After some time he was, at his own solicitation, named to a post in the army, and one day he secretly, without rhyme or reason, fled and took sanctuary in the British mission. Mr. Thomson wished to appoint him first Persian secretary to the mission, and intimated his nomination to that post to the Persian ministers; but they

[a] Meerza Hashem Khan never was named to any post in the army.—[This and the notes marked "*M.*" on the succeeding pages, are by the Hon. C. A. Murray.]

silenced him by sound arguments, and he relinquished his first intention, when he dismissed him from the situation and placed another in his stead, whose appointment he announced to the Persian government. The Persian authorities desired to withdraw Meerza Hashem Khan from the sanctuary of the mission; but he put off from day to day, saying that he feared he would be molested. Mr. Thomson proposed to send him to the Persian ministers, accompanied by one of his own people; but the Persian ministers declined, because several cases similar to this had occurred, and whenever a person from the mission came along with any one, he was considered by the mission as one of their dependents and a British subject. Mr. Thomson was informed that if Meerza Hashem Khan left the mission without the interference of the British authorities, he would be treated with perfect kindness. He, however, remained in the mission until Mr. Murray arrived, and in the summer, when the shah with his court and the mission all removed to their summer quarters, Meerza Hashem Khan accompanied the mission.

"From what we have heard from Persia, whether true or false we cannot assert, Meerza Hashem Khan, who is married to the daughter of one of the princes, and about whose wife there is a long story which cannot be inserted in this paper, took his wife with him to the summer residence, and gave her a place near the garden in which Mr. Murray resided.[b] This matter having acquired in the city of Tehran notoriety in an improper and scandalous way, it appears that the Persian ministers, wishing to make (Mr.) 'Murray' acquainted with this circumstance, addressed an official letter to him and to the other foreign missions in Tehran; and, under a disguise, explained the matter to them all in general terms, intending that (Mr.) Murray[c] should be warned, and alter his conduct so that mischief should not be excited for himself and the Persian

[b] The Meerza took his wife with him when he accompanied the mission to country quarters, and as the whole village does not contain more than thirty houses, it is not wonderful that theirs should be near the garden in which Mr. Murray resided.—*M.*

[c] Throughout the rest of the paper, her majesty's minister is mentioned as "Murray," without any titles whatever.—*M.*

ministers.[d] (Mr.) Murray paid no attention to these hints, and when he returned to Tehran, he again hired a house in the neighbourhood of the mission for the wife of Meerza Hashem Khan.[e] The priesthood and people of Tehran,[f] on learning this, sent letters and wrote petitions on the score of religion, and expostulated with the Persian ministers, and, as nearly as possible, they were having a sudden and general tumult. (Mr.) Murray seeing that the curtain was withdrawn, began a discussion and correspondence with the Persian ministers, under the pretext that he in-

[d] This circular addressed to the missions had no reference at all to the British mission, and was antecedent in date to all the discussions concerning Meerza Hashem Khan and his wife.—*M.*

[e] A downright falsehood. She lived with her own husband, and Mr. Murray did not and does not even know where their house was situated.—*M.*

[f] "The priesthood, &c.," that is, the Sadr Azim himself, drew up a paper containing all his own calumnies and falsehoods, and sent it round among the priests, requiring them to affix their seals to it, which many of them, for fear of his displeasure, were obliged to do. The chief priest, Imaum-o'-Joomab, had the courage to refuse to sign the paper, saying that he had no knowledge of the truth of its contents.—*M.*

tended to employ Meerza Hashem Khan in the mission, and to send him to Fars. Notwithstanding all the remonstrances made by the Persian ministers, who demanded by what right or on what grounds he appointed a servant of the shah, who had been brought up in the royal family, to the mission, he would not listen; and, not satisfied with persisting in his demands, he alluded to the wife of Meerza Hashem Khan openly and publicly in an official letter, and demanded and intended to compel the Persian ministers to lend themselves to the disgrace and danger of sending Meerza Hashem Khan's wife to the mission.[g] They, however, perceiving how dangerous the matter was, could not consent to his proposition, and (Mr.) Murray made this the pretext for striking the mission flag, for suspending relations, and for withdrawing the mission towards the Turkish territory. Our correspondent writes that it is extraordinary indeed

[g] Another gross and absurd falsehood. Mr. Murray's demand, often repeated and transmitted to the Foreign Office, was that she should be released, and be restored to her husband.—*M.*

that this affair in a Mahometan country did not lead to a general outbreak and tumult; and that the Persian ministers must have taken great trouble in preventing things from going further. From what our correspondent hears, if Mr. Thomson struck the mission flag, still it was on account of a merchant, and was not so disgraceful: but it is very disgraceful that the English flag should come down for the sake of a woman. We do not know in what way the British government will remove this disgrace, or how they will treat their representative.

"Our correspondent has also learned that Dost Mahomed Khan, the ruler of Cabul, had marched, at the instigation of the English government, and with their support, against Candahar, and had captured that place; and that he intended to take Herat also. Although our correspondent was not certain of the truth of this intelligence, if such should really prove to be the case, it is evident that the withdrawal of the English mission from the capital of Persia has been planned on that account;[h]

[h] The flag was hauled down, and the mission removed

otherwise, a matter of so little importance as that reported to us, and which is the ostensible reason for the removal of the mission from Tehran as stated above, could hardly have caused a rupture in the relations of that friendship which has for so many years existed between the government of England and that of Persia. This is a rumour which has reached our correspondent; but the truth or inaccuracy of it has not yet been ascertained."

The fact that the conduct of nearly all the representatives of England should have proved so distasteful to the Persian authorities, justifies the suspicion that the blame in a great measure rests with the latter. The intemperate language used by the shah himself seems to favour this conclusion. In a note to Sadr Azim, written in December, 1855, the Persian sovereign says:—" Last night we read the paper written by the English minister plenipotentiary, and were much surprised at the rude, unmeaning, disgusting, and insolent tone and purport. The letter which he before

from Tehran, before the news of Dost Mahomed Khan's march had reached that city.—*M.*

wrote was also impertinent. We have also heard that, in his own house, he is constantly speaking disrespectfully of us and of you, but we never believed; now, however, he has introduced it in an official letter. We are, therefore, convinced that this man, Mister Murray, is stupid, ignorant, and insane; who has the audacity and impudence to insult even kings. From the time of Shah Sultan Hossein (when Persia was in its most disorganized state, and during the last fourteen years of his life, when, by serious illness, he was incapacitated for business) up to the present time, no disrespect towards the sovereign has been tolerated, either from the government or its agent. What has happened now, that this foolish minister plenipotentiary acts with such temerity? It appears that our friendly missions are not acquainted with the wording of that document: give it now to Meerza Abbas and Meerza Malcum, that they may take and duly explain it to the French minister and Hyder Effendi, that they may see how improperly he has written. Since last night till now our time has been passed in vexation. We now command you, in order that you may yourself know and also acquaint the missions, that until the queen* of England herself makes us a suitable apology for the insolence of her envoy, we will never receive back this her foolish minister, who is a simpleton, nor accept from her government any other minister."

Towards the end of 1855 the intention of the Persian government to break faith with England in the matter of the agreement signed in 1853, with reference to Herat, became apparent. In December Prince Sultan Moorad Meerza set out from Tehran to put himself at the head of an expedition of nine thousand men, intended to act against Herat. Prince Mahomed Youssuf had, without the aid of Persia, recovered the throne of Herat; but having been threatened by a hostile party in Herat and an attack from Dost Mahomed Khan, he applied to Persia for aid. In a circular addressed by Sadr Azim to the foreign missions in Tehran, dated February 27, 1856, the Persian prime minister detailed his reasons for this offensive movement. Anxiety for the

* The objectionable term "Malikeh" is used.

tranquillity of Khorassan, Seistan, Belooch-istan, and Kerman, and a desire to frustrate the schemes of Dost Mahomed Khan, were the pretexts put forth for this intervention.

In April, 1856, the Persian *chargé d'affaires* at Constantinople again applied to Lord Stratford de Redcliffe on the subject of a settlement of the difficulty; and during the interview he expressed the willingness of the shah to receive Mr. Murray. On the 15th of May Lord Clarendon wrote, in reply to Lord Stratford de Redcliffe's request for instructions, that, with respect to the satisfaction required before Mr. Murray could return to Tehran, her Majesty's government demanded the following conditions: — "That the Sadr Azim should write a letter to Mr. Murray, expressing his regret at having uttered and given currency to the offensive imputation upon the honour of her Majesty's minister, and requesting to withdraw his own letter of the 19th of November and the two letters of the minister of foreign affairs of the 26th of November, one of which contains a rescript from the shah repeating the imputation upon Mr. Murray. That in the same letter the Sadr Azim should declare that no such further rescript from the shah as that was communicated, directly or indirectly, to any of the other foreign missions at Tehran; and that a copy of the Sadr Azim's letter, containing this apology and declaration, should be officially communicated by the Sadr Azim to each of the foreign missions at Tehran; that the original letter should be transmitted to Mr. Murray, at Bagdad, by the hands of some high Persian officer, and should be accompanied by an invitation to Mr. Murray, in the name of the shah, to return with the mission to Tehran, another person of suitable rank being appointed to conduct him as mehmandar on his journey through Persia. That Mr. Murray, on approaching the Persian capital, should be received by persons of high rank deputed to escort him into the town and to his residence; and that, immediately on his arrival, or, at all events, at noon on the following day, the Sadr Azim should go in state to the residence of the British mission, and personally renew friendly relations, and should then accompany him to the presence of the shah."

Little was known in Asia of the fall of Sebastopol, but the apparent triumph of Russia at Kars, in November, 1855, had been magnified in every possible manner. The news circulated rapidly throughout Asia, and emboldened the Persians, then wholly under Russian influence. The expedition against Herat proceeded on its march, the Heratees were defeated near Ghorian, which fort was immediately garrisoned by Persian troops, and Herat was besieged.

Up to this period, the English government fully approved of the proceedings of its agents, supported their actions, and seconded their efforts. A remarkable change, however, took place, with respect to their demands. On the 15th of June, Lord Clarendon wrote to Lord Stratford de Redcliffe, "On condition that Herat is immediately evacuated by the Persians, your excellency need not insist upon sending Meerza Hashem to Shiraz." This concession did not, however, produce the desired effect; and on the 11th of July, Lord Clarendon wrote to the Persian prime minister, to inform him, that unless reparation was promptly made for the breach of agreement and act of hostility in occupying Herat, and the Persian troops at once withdrawn from the city and territory of Herat, the British government would adopt other measures. Instructions were soon after sent out to the Governor-general of India, to collect at Bombay an adequate force of all arms, provided with the necessary means of transport, for occupying the island of Karrack and the city and district of Bushire, and to hold such force in readiness to depart from Bombay at the shortest notice.

Lord Clarendon's ultimatum was delivered to the Persian *chargé d'affaires* at Constantinople. It was couched in these terms:—

"The Sadr Azim to write in the shah's name a letter to Mr. Murray, expressing his regret at having uttered and given currency to the offensive imputations upon the honour of her Majesty's minister, requesting to withdraw his own letter of the 19th November and the two letters of the minister for foreign affairs of the 26th of November, one of which contains a rescript from the shah respecting the imputation upon Mr. Murray, and declaring in the same letter that no such further rescript from the shah as that inclosed herewith in copy was communicated, directly or indirectly, to any of the foreign missions at Tehran. A copy of this letter to be communicated officially by the Sadr Azim to each of the foreign missions at Tehran, and the substance of it to be made public in that capital. The original letter to be conveyed to Mr. Murray at Bagdad by the hands of some high Persian officer, and to be accompanied by an invitation to Mr. Murray, in the shah's name, to return with the mission to Tehran, on his Majesty's assurance that he shall be received with all the honours and consideration due to the representative of the British government—another person of suitable rank being sent to conduct him, as mehmandar, on his journey through Persia. Mr. Murray, on approaching the capital, to be received by persons of high rank deputed to escort him to his residence in the town. Immediately on his arrival there, the Sadr Azim to go in state to the British mission and renew friendly relations with Mr. Murray, leaving the secretary of state for foreign affairs to accompany him to the royal palace, the Sadr Azim receiving Mr. Murray, and conducting him to the presence of the shah. At noon on the following day, the British flag to be hoisted under a salute of twenty-one guns, and the Sadr Azim to visit the mission immediately afterwards, which visit Mr. Murray will return, at latest, on the following day before noon. Satisfaction being thus given, and friendly relations restored, the settlement of the questions of Herat, of Meerza Hashem and of his wife, remains to be stated. Should Herat be occupied by the shah's troops, his Majesty to engage to withdraw them without delay. Should that city be in any way menaced, though not occupied, by the shah's troops, his Majesty to engage not to allow them to occupy it on any account. In either case, the engagement being solemnly given, the British mission to defer to his majesty's wish, if renewed, respecting Meerza Hashem, by not insisting on his appointment at Shiraz; the Meerza's wife, however, to be restored to him, and himself to enjoy the security, emoluments, and position offered by the Persian government in a former stage of the question. The whole of the correspondence respecting Meerza Hashem may then be mutually withdrawn and cancelled; it being to be understood, that no objections will be made by the Persian government to the appointment, as heretofore, of a British correspondent at Shiraz, till that and other matters can be finally arranged by a suitable convention."

The Persian government persisted in its obstinate course, and further discussions and complications were caused by an insult offered to Meerza Mootallib, the Persian writer of the British consulate at Tehran, and the violation —at the instigation of Syed Morteza—of the right of asylum accorded to the residence of the British mission at Tehran. This was done towards the end of May. Other indignities against the British officials were offered, and a rupture seemed inevitable.

On receiving an intimation of the preparations of England, the Persian prime minister gave orders for the increase of the Persian troops in the provinces threatened. On the 22nd of September Lord Clarendon wrote to consul Stevens:—

"I have to acquaint you that orders will be sent to India, by the mail of the 26th instant, to dispatch without further delay to the Persian Gulf, and with a view to operations against the Persian territory, a naval and military expedition for which preparations have been some time in progress. Her Majesty's government consider, therefore, that the time has arrived for the withdrawal from Persia of her Majesty's consuls at Tehran and at Tabreez; and you will accordingly, as soon as possible after the receipt of this dispatch, set out for Bagdad, taking with you the public archives, and breaking up altogether, on your departure, her Majesty's consulate. You will, however, make the best arrangement in your power for the preservation of the mission premises and the property which may necessarily be left behind.

"On the eve of your departure, you will acquaint the minister for foreign affairs that you have been instructed to quit Persia in consequence of the course which the Persian government persists in following with regard to Herat and other matters in discussion between Great Britain and Persia; and you will understand that you are not to be induced, by any assurances tendered to you by the Persian government, to abstain from commencing your journey to Bagdad as soon as you are ready to set out.

"You will acquaint any British subjects who may be at Tehran with your approaching departure, and, if they determine to accompany you, you will permit them to do so; or, if they prefer to remain, you will request the French minister to protect them during the absence of the British mission from Persia. You will be careful not to give to any person whatever the slightest intimation of the intention of her Majesty's government to have recourse to coercive measures in the Persian Gulf.

"It is not intended, at present, to withdraw the East India Company's agent at Bushire, as the presence of the British force in the Gulf will be sufficient to protect him from insult or injury; though, if he has reason to apprehend danger before the force arrives, he will have permission to place himself and his establishment in safety."

On the 24th of September the president of the Board of Control was requested to forward to India, by the next mail, orders for the dispatch of the expedition prepared for operations in the Persian Gulf.

The Persian ambassador, Ferokh Khan, arrived at Constantinople, with full powers to settle all questions in dispute between England and Persia, on the 17th of October. Lord Stratford de Redcliffe was directed to enter into communication with this person. After some negotiation, Ferokh Khan signed a declaration consenting to the immediate evacuation of Herat by the Persian troops, and expressing his readiness to enter into a satisfactory arrangement concerning the payment of compensation for the damage done to the people of the city. On the 22nd of November, the following ultimatum was presented to Ferokh Khan:—

"1. Persia engages immediately to withdraw all the Persian troops from Herat and its territory, and to pay compensation for all damages done by them therein. 2. Persia shall enter into a formal treaty with England, by which Persia will renounce all pretensions of any kind to interfere in the affairs of Herat, or of any portion of Afghanistan; will engage not to receive, at any time, overtures to interfere in their internal affairs; will recognize their absolute independence; and will agree to refer to British mediation any differences which Persia may hereafter have with them. 3. Persia shall negotiate and conclude a new treaty of commerce with England, by which all questions which have hitherto given rise to discussion between the two governments shall be settled, and the right be conceded to England of appointing consuls in any part of Persia. 4. All debts due to British subjects shall forthwith be paid, and an understanding come to on disputed claims. 5. Persia shall make an arrangement respecting Bender Abbas, satisfactory to the Imaum of Muscat, the friend of England. 6. His Majesty, the shah, in consideration of the part taken by the Sadr Azim in the late differences between the two countries, shall dismiss him, and replace him by a minister more likely to maintain a good understanding between England and Persia.

"Upon the conclusion and ratification by the shah of these engagements as regards Herat and Afghanistan, and the withdrawal of the whole of the Persian troops within the frontier of Khorassan—and upon the solemn engagement, under the seal of his Majesty, that (the sixth condition having been complied with) the remainder of the conditions shall be carried into effect six months after the return of the British mission to Tehran, and that the return of the mission shall be attended with all the apologies and ceremonies already specified, except those which the removal of the Sadr Azim renders impracticable—the British mission will return to Tehran, and the British forces will be withdrawn from the Persian territory within a period not exceeding six months after the return of the mission."

In the meantime the news of the capture of Herat arrived at Constantinople. Ferokh Khan accepted the terms of the ultimatum sent by Lord Stratford de Redcliffe to the Persian *chargé d'affaires* during the summer. The firing of twenty-one guns in the Persian capital was represented to be the special right and privilege of royalty and some hesitation was expressed on this point, and the return of Meerza Hashem to Shiraz was next discussed. Lord Stratford de Redcliffe, in a despatch to Lord Clarendon on the 12th of December, admitted that the demand for the dismissal of Sadr Azim was a great obstacle to an accommodation. These protracted negotiations were continued, but they proved fruitless. Three proclamations declaring war against Persia were issued by the Governor-general of India, on the 1st of November; and when the news of this arrived Ferokh Khan declared his engagements null and void, and quitted Constantinople towards the end of December, 1856.

CHAPTER V.

The Second Division in Persia—Opening of the Campaign.

WAR having been decided upon, naval and military expeditions were despatched to the Persian Gulf. One of these—in which the gallant Havelock, whose heroic achievements in India have since made his name a household word amongst us, took part—is described in these pages. The author went through the campaign, of which he gives the following account:—

Major-general Sir James Outram, K.C.B., of the Bombay army, having arrived in India from England, with instructions to assume the chief command and direct the operations in Persia, shortly after the fall of Bushire—the following troops were placed at his disposal by the Bombay government:—14th King's Light Dragoons, one troop of horse artillery, two field-batteries, one thousand Jacob's Scinde horse, 78th Highlanders, 23rd Native Light

Infantry, 26th Native Infantry, and a light battalion, composed of ten light companies of different native infantry regiments not employed with the field force.

These troops were organized as the second division of the army in Persia on the 10th January, 1857, when Sir James Outram was gazetted in orders, with temporary rank as lieutenant-general while employed, to command in chief. Major-general Stalker, C.B., remained in command of the first division, then in Persia—with Brigadier Wilson, her Majesty's 64th regiment (who had replaced Brigadier Stopford of the same regiment, killed in action,) and Brigadier Honnor, 4th Bombay rifles, commanding the two infantry brigades of that division—Brigadier Tapp the cavalry, and Brigadier Trevelyan the artillery. Brigadier-general Havelock, C.B., deputy-adjutant-general of her Majesty's forces in India, was appointed to command the second division, with Brigadier Hamilton, 78th Highlanders, and Brigadier Hale, Bombay army, for its two brigades. These were composed as follows:—First brigade: 78th Highlanders; 26th regiment, native infantry: second brigade: 23rd regiment, native light infantry; the light battalion. Brigadier-general Tarol, C.B., the highly reputed chief of the Scinde horse, commanded all the cavalry of both divisions; and Colonel Stuart, 14th light dragoons, as brigadier, that of the second; Brigadier Hill having the artillery.

Of these troops the 78th Highlanders, then quartered at Poona, were moved at once on the presidency for embarkation, marching in two divisions; the first (their left wing) quitting Poona at eight hours' notice, on the morning of 7th January, 1857; the head-quarters and right wing following the succeeding day. The entire regiment, under Colonel Histed's command, was halted at Khandalla from the 10th until the 18th of January, waiting till the transports were in readiness, and it lost one corporal and a private from exposure to the sun. The different native infantry regiments of the division were all in motion about the same period at the different ports selected for their embarkation.

On the morning of the 18th, the head-quarters wing of the Highlanders marched to Campoolee, at the bottom of the Bhore Ghaut, and were conveyed thence to Bombay by railway, embarking at once on the Peninsular and Oriental Company's steamer *Precursor*. The left wing of the regiment, commanded by Major McIntyre, followed on the succeeding day, and was embarked on the steamer *Pottinger*, belonging to the same company; but had the light company, under Captain Hunt, detached on board the transport *Kingston*.

On the afternoon of the 19th, the ships put to sea, the *Precursor* having in tow the ships *Earl of Clare*, with the 26th regiment, native infantry, on board; and *British Queen*, with artillery, stores, &c., &c. The *Pottinger* towed the transports *Futteh Mombarrak*, with horses, forage, &c., &c., and the *Kingston*, with the light company of the 78th Highlanders; all the ships getting well clear of the harbour before nightfall.

About daybreak on the 27th of January the land was made, at the mouth of the Gulf of Ormuz, without any occurrence worthy of remark after leaving Bombay, unless parting company with the *Precursor* and her ships in tow, during the night of the 26th, may be noticed as such.

On the 28th the ships were off Bassadore, and about mid-channel between the Arabian and Persian coasts, which in the narrowest portions of the entrance to the gulf are not more than twenty-four or twenty-five miles apart. The land on both sides presents a most dreary and barren appearance; high, precipitous cliffs, of brownish-grey colour, rising sheer from the water's edge, without sign of vegetation or human abode. Many rocky islands of the same desolate description as the mainland stud both coasts; and, were it not for the occasional sight of boats in shore, the whole country on either side might be supposed to be uninhabited. The features of the high lands on both sides bear great resemblance (except in colour) to those of the Red Sea. The few boats we met were evidently careful to avoid the shipping, and invariably kept close in to the land on its first appearance.

About noon on the 30th of January, the French frigate *Sibylle*, fifty guns, commanded by Captain Maisonneuve, was signalled to windward; she having left Bombay about eight days before the squadron, on a mission to the Gulf to protect French interests, and show the Persians that the *entente cordiale* between France and Great Britain was still uninterrupted. This sloop, although heavily armed, appeared to be a dull sailer, and had anything but the smart appearance of ships of her class of the present day. Her being painted in mourning may have, in some measure, added to this—the remains of Captain Maisonneuve's father being on board for conveyance to France. He had formerly been governor of Pondicherry and commander-in-chief of all the French possessions in India, and died at Bombay some thirty years back. On the disinterment of the remains at the Roman Catholic cathedral, where they had so long rested in the "Girgaune" grove, every ceremonial of respect had been observed, and they were removed in solemn procession, and with all military honours, on board the frigate, the governor and officers of the garrison attending in compliment to our allies.

Bushire was sighted about two o'clock the same afternoon, and the anchors were down in the roadstead before dark, immediately after which orders were received to disembark the troops on the following morning, in light marching order, with no baggage except their bedding, which in Indian regiments consists of a settringee, or cotton padded rug, and a pair of blankets.

The left wing of the Highlanders, having arrived before the *Precursor* with the head-quarters, were accordingly disembarked the succeeding day, and marched into the entrenched camp, occupying an outwork to the left front of the lines of her majesty's 64th regiment. The head-quarters followed on the 31st, accompanied by the 26th native infantry, —all received with almost an excess of hospitality, both officers and men, by the force in camp; soldiers of different companies of both the 64th and 2nd light infantry (Bombay Europeans) sending their rations of porter or spirits as presents to their namesake companies of the Highlanders; and the first division officers, finding that their comrades of the second had been landed without aught but the clothes they wore, and were, equally with their men, dependent upon the commissariat, proved good Samaritans indeed, and established a feeling which those who experienced their good fellowship will not readily forget.

The entrenchment round the camp was a simple ditch about three feet deep and six in width, with a parapet composed of what earth had been dug out;—flanking batteries at the angles and salient points. The camp itself, situated rather more than a mile outside the town, stretched across the isthmus, and faced to the village of Bushire. None of the enemy having been seen in its neighbourhood since the capture of the town, a cavalry picket, about two miles to the front, was the only outpost duty.

Bushire itself is a place of much importance, and covers considerable ground. It is defended by a wall (but of no great thickness) with round towers at about musket-range intervals, for flank defence, and has no ditch. As a fortress it is inconsiderable—position and trade giving it all its value; and yet, as a

G. H. H, del. — E Walker, Lith.   George Routledge & Co. London & New-York.   Day & Son, Lithrs to the Queen.

ENTRENCHED CAMP & TOWN, BUSHIRE

commercial town, none in the world has perhaps been oftener attacked. It is no uncommon occurrence for its own governor to hold out in opposition to the shah, and, on a matter of tribute or taxes, set his arms and authority at defiance; and no later than eight or nine years ago such was actually the case.

Situated on a sandy spit, the sea washing two faces and a swampy creek a third, it is a dreary desolate-looking spot at all times; and yet from the harbour, owing to the solid and square appearance of the buildings, the town has a look of importance which its reality, on visiting, at once belies. It is chiefly composed of narrow, blind alleys for thoroughfares, with filth and mud *ad libitum*. The Armenian church within its walls is worth a visit, as also the bazaar, and a very extraordinary water reservoir opposite to the residency. The Halilah Peak and ranges of hills in the back ground are very abrupt and bold, the higher ridges at this season capped with snow. The climate is most delightful, but the nights are bitterly cold.

Sir James Outram had arrived some days

before the Highlanders, and not being a man likely to keep the troops in idleness, all manner of rumours as to future operations circulated in the camp. Among the most prominent were an attack upon the entrenched camp at Brásjoon, about fifty miles distant, where the enemy were in force; and the capture of Mahommern, a fortified place, strongly occupied, some two days' sail distant on the Euphrates; but, though much was talked of about both these affairs, nothing was certainly known.

Supplies of all descriptions were plentiful and good in camp, and the inhabitants both of the town and neighbourhood were evidently pleased at the British occupancy; indeed, they could scarcely be otherwise; for, irrespective of the pecuniary advantages of the presence of a large force which paid heavily and on the spot for everything, the orderly look and appearance of the soldiery who visited the town, without even side-arms as a protection to themselves or as a threat to overawe, contrasted most advantageously with the previous garrison, which, irregularly paid, and that at very long intervals, had notoriously lived upon what could be extracted or stolen from either the citizens or the neighbouring tribes coming into the market.

The Highlanders, and indeed the remainder of the second division, having landed without tentage, the commissariat provided sufficient for temporary accommodation, but not for comfort, thirty men being stowed in each of the soldiers' tents, and two officers and their servants had to accommodate themselves as best might be in a rowtee tent some ten feet by eight.

The expectation of being soon actively employed was fully confirmed. On the afternoon of the 3rd of February, at six o'clock, the entire force (excepting a sufficient guard for the camp, to assist which a party of seamen from the ships of war were landed to serve as artillerymen) was drawn up outside the entrenchments in the following order:—two lines of contiguous quarter-distance columns. First line: first brigade, first division — her Majesty's 64th regiment and 20th regiment native infantry. First brigade, second division—78th Highlanders and 26th regiment native infantry. Second brigade, first division—2nd European light infantry and 4th Bombay rifle regiment, native infantry. Second line: 3rd light cavalry (two squadrons); 3rd (Blake's) troop horse artillery; Nos. 3 and 5 field batteries; one rissalak of Poona horse. An advance guard was formed seven hundred yards on the right of all under Colonel Tapp, of the Poona irregular horse, composed of one troop 3rd light cavalry, two guns horse artillery, two companies of her Majesty's 64th regiment, and two companies of 20th regiment native infantry; the rear-guard, under Major Hough, consisting of his own, the 2nd Belooch battalion, and one troop of Poona horse, was drawn up on the left.

On being joined by Sir James, the army moved off, and, marching all night with nothing but the usual occasional halts, reached Char-Kota, a village about twenty-six miles distant, by nine o'clock on the morning of the 4th. Here a halt was called for the remainder of the day, the different regiments piling arms in column in the same order as they had marched, and the men lying by them.

The road traversed had been round the head of the Bushire creek, and was alternately hard and loose sand, and reedy swamp, a small fortified tower near some wells and a few scattered date trees being the only objects of interest passed upon the march.

During the halt great discomfort was experienced from a very high wind, which enveloped the country for miles around in one huge cloud of sand, forcibly reminding those who had experienced them of the Aden "shimauls," and rendering utterly useless what little cover the few stunted trees in the neighbourhood afforded. At four o'clock in the afternoon the march was resumed; and as a cavalry picket of the enemy had occupied Char-Kota but a few hours before our arrival, the arms were loaded before moving off. At ten o'clock at night the column halted, having accomplished about fourteen miles, and being supposed to be distant about eight miles from the enemy's position.

Here the men bivouaced in order of march, and had scarcely lain down, when a terrific thunderstorm, with hail and heavy rain, broke, drenching all to the skin, and with a piercing cold wind blowing, rendered the night one of great hardship to all, passed as it was by men and officers alike, without cover of any kind. All rejoiced when the rouse sounded on the morning of the fifth; and, knowing the proximity of the enemy, were in high spirits at the expectation of a brush with him during the day. Before quitting the bivouac, to avoid mischances from the night's heavy rain, the loaded arms of the day previous were fired, and freshly charged. By eight o'clock the force was again in motion, and the march directed on the position at Brásjoon, where the enemy were said to be entrenched and to have eighteen guns.

The country passed over was much of the same description as that previously seen, but the nearer approach enabled one to form a more correct estimate of the great height and formidable, bold character of the surrounding hills. They are in truth, excepting at the two or three routes, or rather pathways, in use utterly impassable; and even on those a handful of determined men might, at every turn of the road, stop an army. The lowlands at the base of the hills are sandy and desert, with here and there patches of palm and date trees and corn cultivation. Just as the force commenced its march, a rumour was in circulation that the hill tribes among the enemy, who are esteemed their stoutest soldiers, had deserted them; but subsequent events proved this to be untrue.

Once in motion, the march became a very rapid one, all being anxious to reach the entrenchments and commence the morning's work. Shortly before one o'clock the Persian *vedettes* and reconnoitring parties were made out, and, on our approach, retired before us. A short halt took place to get the regiments into their different positions for attack, when, to the disgust of all, the entire army in our front was descried in full retreat, and going off at such a pace as to render it hopeless attempting to overtake them. A smart brush, however, took place between their rear-guard and a few of our cavalry, in which an officer* and two or three troopers

* Cornet Spens, 3rd light cavalry.

received some slight wounds. Brigadier Honnor also narrowly escaped severe injury, a bullet passing through his clothes and lodging in the tree of his saddle.

By two o'clock our force was in possession of their entrenched camp, and great quantities of ammunition of all kinds, together with grain and camp equipage, fell into our hands, the enemy having gone off in a most hurried and disorderly manner. The entrenched camp was outside the village of Brásjoon, and of itself was a most miserable defence, being perfectly practicable for cavalry to ride over at nearly all points, while, on the contrary, the village in its immediate neighbourhood might have been made even too formidable a post for our small army to have attempted. A wall, with tower bastions at intervals, enclosed the whole, and detached square towers within overlooked all. A ditch fifteen feet deep ran round the outside, and beyond it gardens, with high thorn and cactus fences. In proper hands the capture of such a place must cost both time and many sacrifices.

The 6th and 7th of February were passed in

G. H. H. del E. Walker lith. George Routledge & Co. London & New York Day & Son, Lithrs to the Queen

the enemy's position, destroying stores and searching for buried guns, which were afterwards ascertained to have been thrown down wells, their carriages and wheels being found by us and burned. Some treasure was also discovered, and many horses and carriage cattle secured. During this time no annoyance was experienced from the enemy, though an alarm on the night of the 6th caused the whole of the troops to stand to arms. From information received afterwards, and their own despatch, this alarm was not altogether a groundless one, as they felt up to our outposts, but finding the troops under arms, and it being a bright moonlight night, they attempted nothing. Many jokes were, however, current in camp next day on the events of the night, the picket of one regiment having taken a DOOR prisoner, which was leaning against a bush in a most suspicious manner; and those of two other gallant corps skirmished up to, and were very nearly having a battle of their own with, a patrol of the Poona horse. However, all passed off without accident. Many spies were doubtless in our camp during the entire period of our stay, and the enemy were well informed of every movement; regardless of which, however, intercourse between the villagers and camp was encouraged, and such strict precautions enforced that they should not be pillaged or ill-treated, that they were civil if not friendly, and at any rate gave no trouble.

At eight o'clock on the evening of the 7th the return march to Bushire was commenced, the column taking with it as much of the captured stores as carriage was procurable for, and the military governor of Brásjoon as a prisoner — this personage proving a double traitor. The general's intention that the return march was to be a leisurely one had been so widely made known through the force, that the stirring events then so shortly to occur were little indeed expected by any one. After moving a few hundred yards clear of the entrenchment, the troops were halted to witness the explosion of a very large quantity of the enemy's powder, stated to be thirty-six thousand pounds, and a most magnificent as well as extraordinary spectacle it occasioned. The evening was darker than usual, and the rush of one mighty column of flame into the heavens, with cloud over cloud of bright silvery-looking smoke, mingled with shells bursting like sky-rockets in the midst, attended by a report that made the hills echo again, and a concussion which shook the ground even where the advance-guard stood, formed altogether an event of life not likely to be forgotten by any who beheld it. The pile of ammunition was fired by Lieutenant Gibbard of the horse-artillery, and Lieutenant Hassard, the adjutant of the 2nd European light infantry, with rifles and shell bullets of Colonel Jacob's invention, from a distance of about one hundred and fifty yards. Both these officers were thrown down by the shock of the concussion. Did any doubt previously exist of the formidable character of this new weapon and projectile, the occurrence described fully removed it. The march was then resumed, and until midnight nothing took place to disturb the usual quiet, orderly movement onwards; indeed, the enemy having been reported as seen the day previously retiring in haste through the mountain-passes, and dragging his guns on sledges over country where it would have been madness to follow him, no idea of his proximity was entertained by any of at least the regimental officers of the army. If the staff possessed better intelligence, it was most religiously kept quiet. Shortly after midnight, however, a sharp rattle of musketry in the rear, and the opening of two horse-artillery guns, put every one on the *qui vive;* and that an attack in force upon the rear-guard was taking place, became apparent to all. The column at once halted, and then moved back to extricate the baggage and protecting troops. These, however, were so ably handled by Colonel Honnor (who was in command) as to need little assistance, save for the increasing numbers of the assailants.

In about half an hour after the first shot was fired, not the rear-guard only, but the entire force, was enveloped in a skirmishing fire. Horsemen galloped round on all sides, yelling and screaming like fiends, and with trumpets and bugles making as much noise as possible. One of their buglers had the audacity to go close to the front of a skirmishing company of the Highlanders, and sound first the "Cease fire," and afterwards "Incline to the left," escaping in the dark. Several English officers having but a few years since been employed in organizing the Persian troops, accounted for their knowledge of our bugle-calls, now artfully used to create confusion. The silence and steadiness of the men were most admirable, and the manœuvring of regiments that followed, in taking up position for the remaining hours of darkness, was as steady as an ordinary parade, and this during a midnight attack, with an enemy's fire flashing in every direction, and cavalry surrounding, ready to take advantage of the slightest momentary confusion. Pride may well be felt in the steadiness of any troops under such circumstances; and how much more so when, as on the present occasion, two-thirds had never before been under an enemy's fire. The horsemen of the enemy were at first very bold, dashing close up to the line, and on one occasion especially to the front of the 78th Highlanders; but finding that they could occasion no disorder, and having been in one or two instances roughly handled by the cavalry and horse-artillery, this desultory system of attack gradually ceased, and the arrangement of the troops for the remainder of the night was effected under nothing more serious than a distant skirmishing fire. The formation adopted was an oblong, a brigade protecting each flank, and a demi-brigade the front and rear, field-battery guns at intervals, and a thick line of skirmishers connecting and covering all; the horse-artillery and cavalry on the flank of the face fronting the original line of march, the front and flanks of the oblong facing outwards; the baggage and followers being in the centre. When thus formed, the troops lay down, waiting for daylight in perfect silence, and showing no fire or light of any kind.

During the completion of these arrangements, Sir James met with a severe accident—his horse falling with, and rolling over, him; but all was so quietly and rapidly carried out by the chief of his staff, Colonel Lugard, that few knew of the mishap until next morning. Scarcely was the formation completed, when the enemy opened five heavy guns, and round shot were momentarily plunging through and over our position—the range of which they had obtained very accurately. Our batteries replied; and this cannonade continued with occasional intervals until near daylight, causing but few casualties, considering the duration of the fire. One shot, however, plunging into the 64th regiment, knocked down six men, killing one of the number; and another, first taking off a foot from Lieutenant Greentree, also severely wounded Captain Mackler, of that regiment. Several of the native followers and baggage animals in the centre were also killed and injured; but the quiet and orderly conduct of the troops doubtless saved them from many casualties; and the musketry-fire having been but seldom replied to after the guns opened, the enemy had no opportunity of improving his original range.

Thus matters continued until dawn, when the Persian fire having for some half-hour slackened, it was currently believed that they would make off; but, to the joy and surprise of all, as the morning mist cleared away, their army was descried in position, fairly offering us battle. They were drawn up in line, their right resting on the walled village of Khoosh-aub and a date-grove, their left on a hamlet with a round fortalice tower. Two rising mounds were in front of their centre, which served as redoubts, and where they had their guns; and they had some deep nullahs on their right front and flank, thickly lined with skirmishers. Their cavalry, in considerable bodies, were on both flanks. Their entire strength was certainly (from the ground they covered) over six thousand infantry and two thousand horse. Sooja-ool-Moolk, reputed to be the best officer in the Persian army, was at their head, and the cavalry were commanded by the hereditary chief of the tribes in person. There was scarcely time to observe their position when the battle began. A sharp cold wind soon cleared away the mist with which the morning of the 8th February opened; and when fairly sighting each other, a rapid cannonade on both sides commenced the battle of Khoosh-aub.

The outward formation of our infantry brigades, to protect the baggage and followers over-night, rendered some manœuvring and a change of front to the original direction of march necessary, as the enemy's line interposed to the north-east. This was soon effected, the regiments countermarching, and deploying on their rear divisions. This, in some measure, transposed the position of brigades, as the first brigade of the first division, which had been, during the night, in advance of the first brigade, second division, was now placed in rear of it; but all the regiments moving up as they successively deployed, two general lines were formed. The front line consisted of the 78th Highlanders and a party of sappers on the right; then the 26th regiment native infantry, the 2nd European light infantry, and the 4th rifle regiment on the left of all. The second line had her Majesty's 64th regiment on its right; then the 20th regiment native infantry, and the Belooch battalion on its left. The light companies of battalions faced the enemy's skirmishers in the nullahs, and covered both flanks and rear of their own army. A detachment of the 3rd cavalry assisted in this duty, and, as the enemy showed some bodies of horse threatening a dash on the baggage or wounded men, these were of considerable service. They had also in their charge the governor of Brásjoon, who—endeavouring to attract attention by placing his black Persian cap on a stick, and waving it as a signal to his countrymen—was immediately, and very properly, knocked off his horse, and forced to remain on his knees until the fortune of the day was decided.

The lines advanced directly the regiments had deployed, and so rapidly and steadily did the leading one move over the crest of a rising ground (for which the enemy's guns were laid), that it suffered but little, the Highlanders not having a single casualty, and the 26th native infantry, their companion regiment in brigade, losing only one man killed, and having but four or five wounded. The first brigade, first division, fared worse, as the shot passing over the regiments then in their front, struck the ranks, and occasioned the greatest loss of the day. The second brigade, first division, suffered equally, but had more killed among their casualties, especially in the 2nd European light infantry.

During this time the cannonade had been continuous; but as the Persian fire in some degree slackened, our artillery advanced to closer action, making most beautiful practice, and almost silencing the opposing batteries. Some bodies of horse soon presented an opportunity for a charge, and the squadrons of the 3rd cavalry and Tapp's irregulars, who had hitherto been on the right front, dashed at them, accompanied by Blake's horse-artillery, and made a sweeping and most brilliant charge, sabring gunners, and fairly driving the enemy's horse off the field. The infantry lines were still advancing rapidly and in beautifully steady order, to sustain this attack, and were just getting into close action, when the enemy lost heart, and his entire line at once broke and fled precipitately. The men cast away their arms and accoutrements, and, as the pursuit continued, even their clothing. Two or three of their sirbar or regular battalions, on their extreme right, alone retired with any semblance of order. The 3rd cavalry were seen to charge through, and back again, one of these battalions, which attempted to receive them with steadiness. Captain Forbes, who commanded the squadrons, was severely wounded; and Captain Moore and his brother, a subaltern of the regiment, both had their horses killed. The Poona horse were by no means behind their cavalry comrades in gallantry, and did their work well. The rout of the enemy was complete; and the troopers, as well as irregulars, were fairly exhausted cutting down the fugitives. The horse-artillery guns, too, following them as long as their horses could go, destroyed great numbers; and the track of the pursuit was thickly marked by slain and wounded. A standard, with a silver hand on the pike-staff, was taken by the irregulars; and when the light cavalry squadrons returned, every trooper was carrying an enemy's musket, and some of them *two*.

Two very handsome 9-pounder brass guns were captured on the field, and remained in our hands. The rest of their artillery was carried off, when they fled at the cavalry charge, their commander-in-chief, Sooja-ool-Moolk, accompanying them.

Their horsemen proved dastardly in the extreme; and although showing in considerable numbers on different parts of the field, as if inclined to attack the rear, and cut up the wounded, never approached near enough to effectually engage the covering skirmishers; and on a successful shot being made by Lieutenant Gillespie, of the 2nd European light infantry, with an Enfield rifle, sighted for eight hundred yards, which emptied one of their saddles, the remainder of the party made off, and did not again show themselves. Their line of retreat lay to the rear of the village of Khoosh-aub, the name of which the general adopted for the action.

More than seven hundred of their dead were left upon the field, with many horses; how many were slain in the pursuit, or died of their wounds, it was of course impossible to ascertain. No great number of prisoners fell into our hands; their own cowardly treachery in many instances, after having received quarter, enraged the men, and occasioned free use of the bayonet. One or two men of consequence were, however, among those taken. These brilliant results were secured with a loss on our part of only one officer and eighteen men killed, and four officers and sixty men wounded. Among the unfortunate camp-followers, however, crowded together during the preceding night-attack, several were killed and wounded, and many not accounted for.

By ten o'clock in the morning, the cavalry and guns had returned from pursuit, and the troops, marching a short distance to the right of the battle-field, bivouacked on the original line of march, the men cooking and refreshing themselves before resuming the route on Bushire. About mid-day heavy rain commenced falling, and continued without intermission for several succeeding days. The condition of the troops, when it had fallen some hours, must be left to imagination. The roads were all but impassable, from sticky mud, half clay and sand, and over ankle-deep; yet, through this, and drenched to the skin, the column marched the entire night of the battle, moving off the field about eight o'clock in the evening. The guide, either from treachery or ignorance, misled the force, and about four in the morning a halt took place in consequence, to wait for daylight. There, in the midst of pitiless rain, sunk knee-deep, and a biting northerly wind, two long weary hours were passed, without a tree even in sight, and the swamp around looking in the hazy light like a vast lake. Yet men and officers alike stretched themselves in the mire, and endeavoured to snatch the rest which the exhausting labours of so many previous hours made a paramount necessity. The troops reached the tower and wells of Chuga-duck, between Char-Kota and Bushire, by ten o'clock; and after a halt until two o'clock the same afternoon (9th), again, in midst of heavy rain, resumed the march on Bushire, which was reached by the infantry column about nine at night. All were, it is true, tired out and fagged, but with spirits undiminished; and not only without leaving a single man to fall into the enemy's hands, throughout the entire expedition, but bringing our slain with us for interment in our own lines. The forty-four miles from the battle-field having been traversed within thirty hours, under the circumstances narrated, renders it needless to say more of the courage and endurance evinced by all.

The horses of both the artillery and cavalry having been so severely worked, both in the action and the pursuit, those arms remained the night at the tower and wells, as did also the rifle regiment and Belooch battalion, and marched into camp on the morning of the 10th of February, amid the hearty cheers of every regiment, justly appreciating their conspicuous gallantry.

On the morning of the 11th, the remains of Lieutenant Frankland, 2nd European light infantry (the only officer killed), and our other slain, were interred together, in presence of the general and nearly every officer of the force. Lieutenant Frankland was acting as brigade-major of cavalry when he met his death, and two or three of the enemy had previously fallen by his hand. His regiment lost in him an officer of great accomplishment, and one generally esteemed. During the day, the following complimentary order was published to the troops:—

"Field Force Order.

"Camp near Bushire,
"Feb. 10, 1857.

"In offering to the troops composing the field force his hearty congratulations upon the successful issue of the operations against the enemy, and especially upon the decisive victory gained over the Persian army under their commander-in-chief, Sooja-ool-Moolk, on the 8th instant, at Khoosh-aub, the lieutenant-general desires to return his sincere thanks to all under his command, for their steadiness and gallantry in the field, their extraordinary exertions on the march, and their cheerful endurance of fatigue and privation under circumstances of peculiar hardship, rendered doubly severe by the inclemency of the weather, to which they were exposed without shelter of any kind. The troops marched from their camp on the evening of the 3rd instant, without tents or extra clothing of any kind, each man carried his great coat, blanket, and two days' cooked provisions. After a march of forty-six miles in forty-one hours, during which they were exposed to the worst of weather, cold winds, and deluging rains, they reached the enemy's irregular infantry, cavalry, and eighteen guns in an intrenched position, on the morning of the 5th, but found it abandoned.

"The enemy, on hearing of our approach, had evacuated their intrenchments so precipitately that their tents and camp-equipage and ordnance magazines were abandoned; the former were being rapidly carried off by village plunderers operating for some hours before we arrived. Every exertion was made to intercept the retreat of some bodies of the enemy's cavalry, and some little skirmishing with a few horsemen took place; but, eventually, they all made off. After occupying for two days the position the enemy had abandoned, and learning that they had succeeded in getting the guns which they had carried away into the difficult pass of Maak, the troops commenced their return march on the night of the 7th instant, carrying away the large stores of flour, rice, and grain, which the Persian government had collected for their army, and destroying their magazine, found to contain about thirty-six thousand pounds of powder, with small-arm ammunition and a vast quantity of shot and shell; and thereby crippling the future operations of their army. Some of the guns are supposed to have been cast into wells, and, as their wheels and carriages fell into our hands, cannot again be used. At midnight an attack was made upon the rear-guard by the enemy's horse, and parties threatened the line of march on every side. The troops were halted, and so formed as to protect the baggage and resist the horsemen in whatever direction they might attempt to charge. Before this was quite completed, four of the enemy's guns, of heavy metal, were opened upon the forces; but the darkness of the night prevented any steps being taken to capture them. At break of day, the Persian force, amounting to between five or six thousand infantry, two thousand and fifty cavalry, and five guns, was discovered on our left rear, north-east of our line of march.

"The cavalry and artillery immediately moved rapidly to the attack, supported by two lines of infantry, a third protecting the baggage and rear. The firing of the artillery was most excellent, and did great execution. The cavalry also charged twice with great gallantry and success; indeed, upon these two arms fell the brunt of the action, as the infantry moved away too rapidly to overtake them. By ten o'clock the defeat of the Persians was complete, and two guns were captured. The gun-ammunition, laden on mules, fell into our hands, and at least seven hundred men lay dead on the field; the wounded—the number of which must have been considerable—were carried away; the remainder fled in a disorganized state, generally throwing away their arms, which strewed the field in vast numbers; and nothing but the paucity of our cavalry prevented their total destruction, and the capture of their remaining guns.

"The troops bivouacked for the day close to the battle-field; and at night accomplished a march of twenty miles over a country rendered almost impassable by the heavy rain which fell incessantly. After a rest of six hours, the greater portion of the infantry continued their march to Bushire, which they reached before midnight on the 9th instant; thus performing another harassing march of forty-four miles under incessant rain, besides fighting and defeating the enemy during the progress, within the short period of thirty hours. The cavalry and artillery, with an infantry escort, reached camp this morning. The result is most satisfactory, and will, the lieutenant-general trusts, have a very beneficial effect on our future operations in Persia. The lieutenant-general therefore feels that he cannot too strongly express the obligation he is under to Major-General Stalker and the officers and men of all arms, for the almost incredible exertions they have undergone, and the gallantry they have displayed on the occasion.—By command,

(Signed) "E. LUGARD, Colonel,
"Chief of the Staff."

For two or three days subsequent to the

return of the troops, the rain continued to fall, and rest was eagerly sought by man and beast, though under circumstances of great discomfort, from the damp of the drenched tents and mud of the encamping-ground. A temporary interval of fine weather ensued for a few days, bringing parades and inspections again to employ all, and strong working parties were furnished by each regiment twice a day to construct five formidable redoubts, four of them in front, and one with a martello tower in its centre, on the rear face of the intrenchment.

Brigadier-General Havelock also arrived at this time and took command of the second division, accompanied by Brigadier Hamilton, who assumed that of its first brigade, which had been held, in the action of the 8th, by Colonel Histed. After the 14th of February several days of rain and unsettled weather again ensued; however, the health and spirits of all continued unimpaired; and occasional races or cricket, during the fine intervals, did much to keep up the prevailing cheerfulness. The supplies brought in had begun

G. H. H. Del. — T. Picken, Lith. George Routledge & Co. London & New York. Day & Son, Lith.rs to the Queen.

ISMAINI, ON THE KAROON

to decrease daily after the action of the 8th, and forage in particular became expensive and scarce; yet the horses of both cavalry and artillery retained condition, and showed but little ill effect from the rough work lately undergone.

The exercise which the working parties, as well as ordinary duties, imposed upon the men, appeared to have a most beneficial effect in a sanitary way, as well as employing their idle time. Three hundred men was the quota furnished daily by every regiment to the engineers for disposal. Heavy surf on the bar of the roadstead now for some days interrupted free communication with the shipping, but preparations steadily continued for what camp rumour affirmed to be a contemplated attack on the town of Mohammerah, a place of some importance situated at the confluence of the Karoon and Euphrates (here called Shāt-el-Arab) rivers, and distant about three days' sail. The enemy being reported to have erected formidable batteries, and to be in considerable force in the place, very serious work was anticipated.

Some companies of the light battalion and guns of the mountain-train joined the force about this time, and the arrival of the 23rd Native light infantry and another troop of horse-artillery, with the cavalry then daily expected from India, would (so said report) be the signal to put all in motion.

The greatest enthusiasm prevailed amongst the different branches of the service, and all seemed anxious to have another conflict with the Persian troops, which they had defeated so easily on a previous occasion; in fact, the hope of getting at the enemy formed the sole topic of conversation amongst members of all ranks.

On the night of the 22nd of February, for the first time since the battle on the 8th, the fires of the enemy were seen on the hills around us; but although the Poona horse pushed their patrols to a very considerable distance, no hostile outpost was encountered. A camp-follower, however, was found murdered and mutilated close to our lines on the following morning. Subjoined is a proclamation from Tehran, in circulation a few days previously, with the royal arms or crest of the shah heading it:—

PROCLAMATION *published at Tehran, on the 26th of the month* RUBBI-OOL-SAMI, *corresponding with* CHRISTMAS-DAY:—

"FROM the commencement of the coolness which has arisen between the British and the Persian governments, the latter has not violated the friendship which previously existed between them, nor evinced any hostility to the British government. As this loyal determination had been acted upon in many recent instances, and had been made manifest to all classes, and had also been published in the *Tehran Gazette*, the Persian government had given power to its great minister at Constantinople to arrange all subjects in dispute with the British ambassador at that court, and thus to remove the coolness which had arisen; and in order to attain this object, he was directed to accede as far as possible to the wishes and requests of the British ambassador: and the hope was confidently entertained that all matters would be arranged in a satisfactory manner by the two great ambassadors, and that the Persian court would be informed of the re-establishment of friendly relations. And, on the other hand, all the authorities on the Persian frontier were directed not to make any preparation for war, nor to attack the British troops. And accordingly, no preparations for war, nor precautions against attack, had been made on the frontier. Among the places in which the above order had been promulgated, was the port of Bushire, in which was only the usual garrison of two regiments; the commander of these also, Colonel Mahomed Ali Khan, had died a few days previously. At this time, the commander of the British troops in the Gulf of Persia—without giving (as is usual) any declaration of war to the Persian government at Tehran, or to the governor-general of Fars—contented himself with sending one copy of a proclamation which had been printed in India, containing a declaration of war with Persia; and this paper, of dubious meaning, was addressed only to Bushire and the neighbouring ports: and on the following day, without granting any delay, he landed his troops from the shipping, and took possession of the fort of Bahrineen [Bushire], which was defended by only a few toofunchees [musketeers] of Tangistoon; and as the garrison of the town had not received the permission of the government to make any resistance to the British troops, they made no effort to oppose them; and thus the British advanced, and entered Bushire without meeting any opposition."

"Translated and signed by

"Captain Rigby, 16th regiment N.I.

"Superintendent of Police, Persian Field Force."

Much was the amusement occasioned by this plausible document, and the apology furnished for surrendering their greatest seaport after a trifling struggle.

CHAPTER VI.

Successful Operations in Persia.

LIFE in camp now became very monotonous, and prevailing high winds caused the greatest annoyance from the drifting sand, which, being of a fineness to penetrate even through the tent-cloths, covered everything with filth, made washing and dressing a misery, and a walk against the wind a downright punishment. These nor-westers, commencing about nine in the morning, usually lasted until sundown, and the delay they necessarily occasioned in the arrival of the transports hourly expected with reinforcements from India, fretted and vexed the general, who was all anxiety for immediate action. Still, though chafed at these untoward circumstances, the troops were not made to suffer (as sometimes occurs) for their leader's disturbed equanimity. Beyond a personal inspection of his entire force, and the presence of division and brigade officers on the private parades of regiments, no extra duties were imposed upon the men, and, to the horror of many a worshipper of the venerated past, the very pipeclay was scrubbed off the belts. Meanwhile, five strong redoubts began to make a formidable appearance—the four in front sweeping the width of the isthmus, and that in the rear securing the communication with the town—all armed with position guns, and one having two 68-pounders. The completion of these works being a material object before the force separated for the projected expedition, the strength of the parties employed upon them still continued as great as before; and, but for the boisterous weather, their erection would have been a popular employment, rather than otherwise, among the men.

Reports were daily current through the camp, of the enemy again appearing in force upon his old ground, and one or two ludicrous incidents occasioned slight alarms, much to the amusement instead of annoyance of all; otherwise things continued as quiet as in ordinary garrison life, until the afternoon of the 4th of

March, when, the wind having lulled on the day previously, and the swell and surf consequently diminished, the embarkation of troops commenced vigorously. Blake's horse-artillery and a field-battery were at once put on board their respective ships, and on the morning of the 5th, the light and No. 8 companies of the Highlanders returned to the transport *Kingston*, preceding the regiment some few days on its voyage to the Euphrates.

It was now known that General Outram's arrangements were to be as follows; viz.—General Stalker to remain in command at Bushire, with Brigadiers Wilson, Honnor, and Tapp; the troops to remain being two field-batteries and the mountain-train, the entire cavalry of the first division, three companies each from her Majesty's 64th and the Highlanders, the 4th rifles, 20th Native infantry, and the Belooch battalion; Sir James proceeding himself with the remainder, to the number, of all arms, of about four thousand men—those left for the defence of Bushire counting about three thousand. The different accounts of Mohammerah stated it to be held by from ten to thirteen thousand men, with numerous cavalry in its neighbourhood and seven of the shah's best regular regiments among its garrison. The works of the fort or batteries were described as very formidable earthen parapets, eighteen or twenty feet thick, with heavy guns on the river face. To encounter these until the troops should land and carry the batteries, were the broadsides of the *Clive* and *Falkland* sloops, and *Ajdaha*, *Feroze*, *Semiramis*, *Victoria*, and *Assaye* frigate steamers; which must, however, face the enemy's fire at the distance of about one hundred yards. The difficulty of the enterprise, however, seemed only the more to determine the general to accomplish it; and camp gossip affirmed that an ill-timed remonstrance from the Turkish government against our attacking a place so near their own (a neutral) territory, had materially hastened our chief's movements, and that the arrival of any portion of the expected cavalry and artillery would be the signal for an immediate advance.

On the 6th of March, before the transport

Kingston put to sea, the *Falkland* sloop sailed for the Euphrates; and about the same time her Majesty's 64th regiment embarked in the *Bride of the Sea* transport; and, even while these events were occurring, the *Feroze*, *Pottinger*, and *Pioneer* steamers entered the roads, bringing a troop of horse-artillery and some of the long looked for Scinde horse; so the departure of the entire expedition now became imminent. Intelligence was also brought in this day, stating so confidently that the new Persian commander-in-chief, with considerable reinforcements, had joined the army recently beaten by us, and intended an advance, that strong hopes, if not actual expectations, were entertained that he might be induced, when the departure of so large a portion of our force became known, to attack the camp and try the strength of our new redoubts, and thus give the troops remaining behind an equal opportunity of honour and distinction with ourselves. On the afternoon of the 6th, the *Kingston*, with four other transports, got clear of the Bushire roads, and were off the island of Karrack early next morning. This formed no exception in desolate rocky appearance to its sister islands in the gulf. A detachment of the 4th rifles held it as a coaling station for the Indian navy. The mouth of the Euphrates was made by daylight on the 8th, with the *Falkland* sloop under all sail leading into it; and after being aground on the bar for about an hour, the *Kingston* anchored by noon among the eight or ten ships that had then arrived—others continuing to reach the anchorage in the course of the day.

A considerable portion of the expedition had assembled in the river, and the cavalry patrols of the enemy evinced great curiosity at our movements, coming down close to the water's edge to make their observations, within easy gun-range; but no shot was fired at them. A day or so previously to our arrival, one of their superior officers held an inspection of about three thousand of their infantry, abreast of the shipping, and evidently intended for observation. A considerable body of their irregulars, both horse and infantry, still occupied the village of Mahamur, opposite to the anchorage, and had pickets established in some ruined buildings within rifle-range. A few of their horsemen occasionally created much interest by tricks of horsemanship and use of weapons, as a show-off before us; but no positive act of hostility, except firing on boats approaching their river-bank too closely, took place.

This branch of the Euphrates, known as the Shāt-el-Arab, is here most uninteresting and ugly; the shores are very low and flat, studded on either side with miserable mud villages, planted in swamp, and backed by thick date-groves. The river itself is about as wide as the Thames at Tilbury Fort, the water very muddy, and with a powerful tideway. The approach to it from the sea is its most extraordinary feature; huge flocks of pelicans and very tall bulrushes giving the first intimation of its proximity. On the melting of the mountain snows, the breadth of the stream is described as being much increased; and as this takes place at the hottest season of the year, and continues but a very few weeks, the subsequent fall of the water leaves a deposit, from which exhalations and malaria arise, causing fever even more deadly than in Scinde. Yet, strange to say, the inhabitants of the river-bank, who have fixed abodes the whole year round, in perfect contrast to the wandering tribes met with further above, are a large, healthy, good-looking race of men. Small-pox, however, would seem to make fearful havoc amongst them, so many of their number bearing the disfiguring traces of this dire disorder. The object of the expedition once attained, the greatest hopes were entertained by all of quitting the marshy neighbourhood before the sickly season should commence.

All landing on either side of the river being positively prohibited—on the enemy's side to prevent loss of life in useless skirmishing, and on the Turkish to preserve scrupulously their neutrality—the interval passed on board ship became irksome in the extreme, and the arrival of the general with the remainder of the force was anxiously looked for, more particularly as the accounts daily received, and reconnaissances made in the little *Comet* steamer, agreed in describing the enemy as still working at defences sufficiently formidable before our appearance in the river, and which, before starting from Bushire, Captain Maisonneuve and our allies of the *Sibylle* had warned us could not be despised, and (from what they had seen during a visit to the place, from which they were just returned) even expressed a conviction that, with our present means, we could not take them. That a general wish therefore prevailed to exchange the idleness on board ship for an active interruption of the Persian industry, may easily be believed.

The head-quarters of the Highlanders arrived in the *Berenice* steamer on the 15th, having also with them Brigadier-General Havelock and the staff of the second division. The regiment had lost one of its young lieutenants from fever (Lieutenant Sinclair) but a day or so before its departure. Wholly unacclimatized, and arrived only a few weeks from England, the climate and exposure proved speedily fatal to the young soldier.

Before night closed on the 16th of March, a troop of the 14th light dragoons and the greater portion of the expected comers were at anchor in the river, and the arrival of Sir James Outram himself was hourly looked for. The *Pioneer* steamer, however, which came in on the following day, brought the melancholy intelligence of the death of Major-General Stalker, by his own hand, at Bushire, and the consequent intention of Sir James to remain there in command, leaving the execution of the projected operations on Mohammerah to General Havelock. One of the troops of horse-artillery, and that of Captain Pretyjohn, of the 14th dragoons, were however ordered to return to Bushire, as the probability of a very serious attack, and in almost overwhelming numbers, threatened when the force left.

A high north-westerly gale setting in, one only of these instructions could be carried out; the horse-artillery, weathering the bar at the river mouth, succeeded in getting back; but the ship carrying the dragoons, striking the mud bank, was fixed there for several days, and then eventually rejoined the second division. Bad weather and sudden changes of arrangement delayed considerably the transhipment of troops, stores, and horses necessary before finally starting to attack; but the transports were all kept busy constructing rafts with casks and spars to disembark the men and horses when required, and the vessels of war in barricading their tops and bulwarks with hammocks and hay-packs, to conceal riflemen and protect their people at the guns.

Matters were thus progressing when, much to the satisfaction of all, Sir James himself, with some Scinde horse and the dragoons he found stuck fast at the mouth of the river, most unexpectedly made their appearance. Signal-books were then eagerly consulted, and many a passing man-of-war's boat hailed for earliest information of the advance up the river.

With Sir James came, however, again, very mournful news—the naval chief, Captain Ethersey, commodore commanding the squadron of the Indian navy serving in the Persian Gulf, having committed suicide at Bushire, by shooting himself, exactly one week after General Stalker's sad example. The fate of these two officers, under such circumstances, and occurring at such a time, caused a feeling of sorrow through the whole force, and almost seemed to portend an evil termination to our enterprise. Both were most estimable members of society and beloved by all who immediately served with them; the one being known throughout Western India as a most popular divisional commander, and a sportsman; the other, as a most amiable and talented officer of great accomplishments. No cause, save over-anxiety, and an oppressive sense of their respective responsibilities, could be assigned as a reason for the rash acts. But a few days of patience and submission were required, and where were the difficulties which induced two such men to rush, uncalled, to their long account?

Until the 23rd of March, all remained quietly at anchor; ships with troops and horses, however, hourly arriving. By the 24th, all were assembled, and on that day ascended the river to the rendezvous appointed, about three miles below the enemy's fortifications, where the final arrangements for attack were to be completed. Besides thick date-groves on either bank of the river, extending some half-mile in shore, and all a sandy flat beyond, no new scenery presented itself; the country, both Turkish and Persian, appearing to be well peopled, and stocked with numerous herds of cattle. The stream was here about three hundred yards in width, yet no attempt was made by the enemy to take advantage of the admirable cover he possessed to annoy the crowded decks so near him; although he evinced great curiosity at our movements, and showed considerable numbers of his men within easy range.

The 25th was occupied in transhipping troops, horses, and guns into the lighter-draught steamers and vessels; but all was completed, and final instructions for the attack given before dark, the blue-jackets of the Indian navy working with a will, and helping their red-coated brethren through every difficulty; the way in which the horses were handled by them being particularly remarked, and the animals themselves seemed to know that they were in proper hands. About nightfall several hundred of the enemy began throwing up an embankment to cover two field-guns which they were seen bringing down; but on the *Assaye* firing some six or eight shells at them, they decamped, not without loss, and the remainder of the night was passed undisturbed. A reconnaissance was made by some engineer officers, who approached the batteries within three hundred yards in a small canoe; and a raft with two eight and two five-inch mortars was established behind a low swampy island in mid-stream, and fronting the enemy's north and most powerful battery.

The cool daring of the men who placed, and the little band of artillery who remained on this raft for several hours of darkness, in the middle of a rapid river, without means of retreat, and certain destruction staring them in the face should the enemy, within but a few hundred yards, be aroused to the fact of their presence—requires no commendation. The simple narrative of the event as it occurred is sufficient.

At daybreak on the 26th of March, the mortars from this raft opened fire, the first shell falling right into the centre of the opposing work, and killing or wounding eleven of the enemy, who, as after-information said, were at prayers at the moment, and in great consternation at not being able to discover for some minutes whence the missile came. The attacking ships got under weigh as the first shot was fired, and proceeded to engage the batteries, going into action as follows:—The *Semiramis*, with the commodore's pendant flying of Captain Young, Indian navy, and towing the *Clive* sloop, led the squadron, followed by the steam-frigates *Ajdaha*, *Feroze*, *Assaye*, and *Victoria*, the latter towing the *Falkland* sloop, which she cast off when in position. The leading ships passing the lower batteries, and opening their guns as they could be brought to bear, were soon at their respective posts, followed in quick succession by the rear division; and but few minutes had elapsed after the *Semiramis* had fired her first gun before the action became general, the Persian artillery replying with great spirit. The morning being very clear, with just sufficient breeze to prevent the smoke from collecting, a more beautiful scene than was then presented can scarcely be imagined. The ships, with ensigns flying from every mast-head, seemed decked for a holiday; the river glittering in the early sun-light, its dark date-fringed banks contrasting most effectively with the white canvas of the *Falkland*, which had loosened sails to get into closer action; the sulky-looking batteries just visible through the grey fleecy cloud which enveloped them; and groups of brightly-dressed horsemen flitting at intervals between the trees where they had their encampment, formed altogether a picture from which even the excitement of the heavy cannonade around could not divert the attention.

The practice from the ships on the enemy's works was most admirable, and the effects of the fire soon became apparent; the embrasures and carefully revetted parapets rapidly losing their original shape, and the crash of the falling date-trees around affording ample proof of the storm of shot. For about three hours the Persian artillerymen stood manfully to their guns; but their fire then slackening, the signal was seen flying for the infantry to move up and disembark. The *Berenice* steamer, carrying the Highlanders, as well as a company of sappers, and General Havelock and the staff of the second division, led the column, her decks crowded to the uttermost, there being barely standing-room for the men on board, and the bridge between her paddle-boxes quite as fully occupied by their officers. The passage of a ship under such circumstances, within one hundred yards of heavily-armed batteries, was an operation attended with great anxiety, which those alone who have been similarly situated can possibly understand. Some of the best troops in the world were helpless for the moment, crowded like cattle in a pen, and so massed that a single round shot must make fearful havoc. The most providential fortune attended the *Berenice;* though struck several times in the hull, and with rigging cut, the decks escaped. Her commander, Lieutenant Chitty, Indian navy, steered the ship himself; and, to avoid all chance of running ashore, and thereby delaying the troops, taking her on the battery side of the first frigate that approached (the *Semiramis*), and between her and the *Feroze.* The crews of these vessels cheered loudly as every fresh freight of red-jackets came up, and while one broadside redoubled its fire to prevent attention to the masses passing, the seamen, jumping on the unengaged guns, let the enemy hear, loud above the roar of the action, their wild welcome to their brethren of the shore.

A desultory matchlock-fire was opened as the spot selected for the disembarkation was approached, which was a few hundred yards above the north battery, on ground comparatively clear of date-trees, though crossed by mud enclosures and intersected by creeks with deep water at high tide. No time was lost in throwing on shore the light company of the Highlanders and the grenadiers of the 64th; on whose advance the enemy's skirmishers at once fell back, and sufficient ground was occupied to secure the further disembarkation from interruption. All the infantry, with a field-battery and some fifty Scinde horse, were on shore by two o'clock in the afternoon, when the rising of the tide having filled the creeks and made impassable the ground to be crossed by the horse-artillery and troop of the 14th dragoons, the general determined on advancing with those who were actually with him.

An immediate move to the front was accordingly made, the 64th grenadiers having to keep down a trifling musketry-fire opened on them while *en route*. At the limit of the date-grove a halt was again called, and the Persian encampments being from this spot plainly in view, Sir James rode up to the front to reconnoitre, and sent the troopers of the Scinde horse, under his military secretary, Captain Green, to examine the position. This was simply two encampments, about five hundred yards distant from each other, to the right and left rear of the town; but in front of them most formidable masses were drawn up when our advance arrived in view. While the troops were landing, and these events occurring, the cannonade between the batteries and men-of-war was still going on. A shell fortunately exploded their grand magazine just as the disembarkation commenced, and their fire gradually slackened; and when the final advance of the troops was made, nothing but a casual gun from the ships was heard.

But while endeavouring to describe the passing scene, and to give the gallant fellows of the Indian navy the credit they so well earned, mention must also be made of the transports, some of which carried a light gun or more. On the troops advancing to disembark, two field-pieces of the enemy came down and opened on the ships abreast. One of these guns remained stationary; the other moved up parallel to the shipping, and gave an occasional shot as the ground proved favourable.

Much mischief might have been occasioned by these, owing to the crowded state of the decks, had not their fire been greatly kept down by those steamers and other vessels which were armed; and the *Pottinger*, especially, was in this way of particular service. She was eight times hulled by the enemy's round shot. As soon as the distances between columns were corrected, which had been unavoidably loosened by the nature of the ground they had come over, and other indispensable arrangements made for the attack, the line advanced, leading direct on the encampment facing it, and before which the greater masses of the enemy were shown.

Our formation was as follows:—a line of contiguous quarter-distance columns; a field-battery on the right. Next came the 78th Highlanders; then the 26th Native infantry (one wing), her Majesty's 64th regiment, the light battalion, and 23rd Bengal light infantry, the whole covered by a cloud of skirmishers. The point of attack was the camp to the left rear of the town of Mohammerah, where the Shah-zadeh had evidently pitched his cavalry and guns, and had been with them in person. His infantry had occupied the other encampment, about five hundred yards to the right of this, and had also been quartered in considerable numbers in the batteries and date-groves adjacent. Up to the moment of our advance, these troops were drawn up, in order of battle, outside the boundary of the Shah-zadeh's camp, the right of their line far outflanking our left, which had actually no protection when it had once advanced into the open plain, beyond the 23rd Native light infantry being slightly thrown back. This great risk, however, caused no hesitation with Sir James. The compact red battalions moved steadily to their front, and the leading skirmishers had arrived within gun-range of the enemy's camp, the field-battery guns actually trotting up to assist them with their fire against the salutes of round shot and grape momentarily expected, when the Persian army seemed literally to have vanished, and, but for the tents still standing, would almost have induced a belief that an illusion of mirage rather than the presence of an armed host had been but so recently before us.

At the last moment all courage had deserted the foe. The lesson of the morning had been too severe to induce even the shah's guards, with his uncle, a prince royal, present at their head, to risk a repetition of the same, although the homes of many and the honour of all their countrymen depended upon the fortune of the day. Their army fled, although the odds were greatly in their favour, and they could hardly expect to meet us under more advantageous circumstances. Every tent was left standing, even that of their prince chief. The ground was strewed with arms, accoutrements, ammunition, band-instruments, saddlery, carpets, grain, bedding, and even their dinners. Many of our round shot, and unexploded shells also, lay around, with bloody proofs of the mischief they had done, and of the tremendous range of the guns they were fired from. Very few of their wounded were found among all this *débris;* so carefully had they either been carried off by their comrades, or concealed by the people of the town close by.

Just previous to their decamping, the runaways blew up their reserve ammunition in one grand mass, as though to throw a veil over their unmanly cowardice. This occasioned some little apprehension that mines might have been left by them to punish and delay their pursuers. All necessary caution was consequently observed on entering their lines, but no halt was made there. Leaving the troops in the rear to secure the property and drive off the Arab marauders, the general moved at once on the track of the flying enemy; but, after continuing the pursuit for three or four miles, and securing only a few of their wounded stragglers, the evening closing in, and no hope of the 14th dragoons or Blake's horse artillery joining before dark, the few troopers of the Scinde horse were left to follow up the track of the retreat, and the halt was sounded for the night.

The troops bivouacked in line of battle where they stood; and the night proving bitterly cold occasioned some suffering to both officers and men, who were without shelter of any kind. An unfortunate groundless alarm took place which induced the outlying pickets of two regiments to fire upon each other, by which five men were wounded, two of them very severely. The dragoons and horse artillery came into camp so soon as the tide permitted their crossing the intersecting creeks, and all were prepared at early dawn to continue the chase; but the return of the Scinde horse, reporting having left the enemy in full flight at eleven miles distance and travelling at a pace hopeless to overtake without strong cavalry, determined the general on first securing and establishing himself at Mohammerah, and breaking up the quarters again of the Shah-zadeh on a future occasion, when the cavalry still expected would give better hopes of accounting for him.

On the 27th, accordingly, the army marched back to Mohammerah, took possession of the town, and occupied the camp of the enemy,—our cavalry and horse artillery going into that of the Persian horse, while the general and staff, with the field battery and one regiment of infantry, occupied the other. The remainder of our infantry bivouacked during the day under the shade of the date-groves, moving out at night to the plain beyond, to escape the chances of malaria arising from the vegetation and muddy creeks; almost intolerable annoyance being experienced from the swarms of flies under the trees by day, and from the myriads of fleas in the sand by night. Guards were immediately posted in the town, and orders issued that private property should be strictly protected, as also every precaution taken to prevent ill-usage to the inhabitants. The result of these measures was that but few hours had elapsed after Mohammerah had changed hands, before perfect confidence prevailed, as well as constant intercourse between the camp and town. The fruits of our victory were now discovered. Eighteen very handsome brass guns and mortars were taken, all in perfect order. One of them was a Russian 12-pounder, cast in 1828, and a present from the late emperor to the shah—at least, so said the inscription upon it. Immense stores of grain, a great quantity of ammunition, many arms and accoutrements, besides the entire tentage of their army, fell into our hands. Many of their dead (some eighty or ninety) lay unburied in the batteries, even though the whole night previous to our entrance the enemy had been employed in burying their slain, as the newly-made graves on the ground outside the date-groves abundantly testified. A loss of three hundred killed was acknowledged by them; but, from the duration of the fire, it must have been greater. Of their wounded but few showed themselves to us, as they had ample time to cross the river (those, at least, able to do so) while we were in pursuit of the retreating army. It would have been better for these unfortunate fugitives had they fallen into our hands, as it was afterwards ascertained that the Arabs mercilessly butchered every one of the helpless wretches that they discovered. The few found by us were taken care of—though so perfectly misunderstood was this kindness at first, that, imagining they were only being reserved for greater torture, they for some time resisted all kind of treatment—even water—from the hands of their captors,—a terrible but unmistakable evidence of their own brutality in warfare. Our own casualties were but ten men killed, and one officer (Lieutenant Harris, I.N.) and thirty men wounded. The officer belonged to the *Semiramis*. This small amount of loss is the more extraordinary as the Persian gunnery was anything but despicable, the ships being hulled in many places by their shot, and rigging cut in all directions, as well as boats smashed; three hundred musket-bullets were also lodged in the broadside of the *Feroze* alone, and many others must also have entered the haypacks by which her sides were protected — these doubtless saved many lives from small-arm fire. The Persian guns got the range of the mortar-raft (a very small object, and about one thousand yards distant) very quickly, striking it once, and also sinking a boat attached to it. Endless tales of hair-breadth escapes also circulated both in camp and on shipboard.

The town of Mohammerah, then in British possession, was found to be a filthy collection of mud buildings, although once a place of considerable trade and importance. Situated at the junction of the Karoon with the Euphrates, it is possessed of every advantage which the water-carriage of two magnificent rivers can give, and is the depôt for all merchandise to or from India for the upper Persian provinces, as well as Bussorah and Bagdad. A rather large and well-supplied bazaar, in the usual Eastern style of filth, and a good-sized garden near the governor's house, are the sole attractions.

In the garden were apple, apricot, and mulberry trees, growing side by side with the plantain, shaddock, and pomegranate, all equally thriving. The country surrounding Mohammerah is alternate swamp or sandy desert, with patches of cultivation, and has the appearance of being annually inundated for miles around, which is actually the case. The date-trees are strictly confined to the belt skirting the river-side, and have but little brushwood or jungle among them. No high land is visible in any direction.

The strength of the batteries was found to have been by no means exaggerated, and considerable skill was displayed both in their position and construction. Nothing but stout hearts within them was required to have made their capture matter of bloody price to the victors: happily for us these were wanting. Solid earth-works, open in rear, with parapets eighteen feet thick and twenty-five feet in height — the embrasures casemated, and revetted with date-stumps (which the heaviest shot will not splinter), and the whole interior thickly studded with pits full of water to catch our shells—had been the work cut out for us. The north battery had embrasures for eighteen guns, and stood on the right bank of the Karoon, at its junction with the Euphrates, and looked across and down the stream of that river. The south battery had eleven guns, and was on the opposite bank of the Karoon, commanding in the same direction. A small fort between the north battery and the town, and connected with the former by a long entrenchment, with embrasures for guns, also mounted eight or ten guns. This entrenchment, crowded with infantry, had kept up a heavy musketry fire during the whole action; and, from the broken pieces of arms and appointments lying about, as well as patches of blood-stains in all directions, our shot must have told fearfully among its occupants.

Several minor batteries of from two to four guns each were on either bank, and just outside the west face of the town, on the right bank, was a very carefully made and strong work for ten guns. The whole of the works bore the marks of very rough treatment from our shot, though they were far from being ruined. Outside the small fort connected with the north battery was a capsized brass 12-pounder, with the carriage smashed, and three dead horses harnessed to it, all evidently killed at the same moment, if not by the same shot. A captain of their artillery and three gunners were also lying dead beside it. A letter found on the officer stated his expectation of a great battle on the morrow, and foreboded his own fate—committing his wife and children to the care of his brother at Tehran. This letter was subsequently safely forwarded to the address it bore by the British political agent at Bagdad.

Two other handsome field-guns and a large brass mortar were found deserted near the brass 12-pounder, the accident to which had prevented the enemy carrying them off; and they must have had some frightful casualties in their ranks while their men were delayed in the attempt. Some few corpses remaining on the spot presented horrible spectacles: a huge African in particular, struck on the back of the head by a round shot which had carried away all the bones of the skull and face, lay across another dead soldier, with the hideous, eyeless black mask that had once been a countenance, still as it were mowing and grinning at the beholder. The scene of the explosion of their grand magazine also afforded some ghastly objects, and the damage it had occasioned was frightful—legs, arms, and heads—wretched mutilated remains of humanity—protruding among the blackened, blasted ruins. The effect of the 68-pounder shot upon the date-trees was most extraordinary, a single one sufficing to snap the largest. The immense size and range of these missiles had occasioned the greatest terror and astonishment among the Persian troops, and doubtless was their excuse for their subsequent dastardly misconduct. Much discouragement was also said to have been created in their ranks by the loss of Agha Jhan Khan, surteep, or general of division, and their most able chief, who fell desperately wounded very early in the day, whilst showing a most gallant example in the north battery.

The 27th and 28th of March were occupied in removing the guns, collecting the stores, &c. &c., and in landing supplies and our own tentage for the troops, who, with the exception of those to whom the Persian tents had fallen prize on occupying their camps, had up to this time been living entirely in the open air.

CHAPTER VII.

Expedition to Akwâz.

DURING the interval, it having been ascertained with certainty that the enemy was directing his retreat on the town of Akwâz, about one hundred miles distant up the Karoon, where he had large magazines and supplies—Sir James Outram decided upon an immediate attempt to be beforehand with him, and, should no very strong garrison have been left in the place, to destroy the stores collected there. For this purpose an expedition was forthwith organized to ascend the river in the steamers *Comet*, *Planet*, and *Assyria*, under the direction of Commander Rennie, of the Indian navy,—an officer who had gained a high reputation in the conduct of similar affairs during the Chinese and Burmese wars, and who was then acting as commodore in command of the squadron in the Gulf, consequent on the departure of Captain Young to India.

The troops told off for the service were, one hundred and fifty men from the flank companies of the 64th regiment, and a like number furnished by the light and Captain McAndrew's companies of the Highlanders. Each steamer took one hundred men, the light companies of the Highlanders going on the *Comet;* Captain Goode's grenadiers, of the 64th, on the *Planet;* and Captain McAndrew, with part of his own Highlanders and part of the light company of the 64th, on the *Assyria.* The expedition was accompanied by the following officers, irrespective of the troops:—Captain Wray, deputy quartermaster-general of the army; Captain Green, military secretary to Sir James; Captain Kemball, political agent and consul at Bagdad; and several other officers.*

The steamers left Mohammerah about ten o'clock on the morning of the 29th of March, the *Comet* leading and lending a tow-rope to the *Assyria,* she being of lesser power; the *Planet* brought up the rear. A gun-boat, carrying two 24-pounder howitzers, was also in

* The author of this work accompanied the Highlanders.

tow of each steamer. Shortly after sunset the flotilla anchored for the night, a little below the ruined fort of Kootul-el-abd, in a very pretty bend of the river. The Karoon is here about one hundred yards wide and from twelve to twenty feet deep, with a powerful current, its banks fringed on both sides with dwarf poplar and willow jungle, which extends but a little distance from the bank. Beyond, nothing is seen but the wide desert, here and there patched with tufts of coarse grass. Such is the prospect far as the eye could reach—the date-trees even ceasing after leaving Mohammerah three or four miles—and no sign of cultivation or human abode appears, to give animation to the dreary wilderness, seldom trodden by the foot of man. Game, however, of many kinds, abounds, and immense flocks of duck and teal are always on the river. The lion, too, is said to be not unfrequently found in the jungle upon the banks.

A party of officers, landing here, found the fires of the enemy's bivouac within fifty yards of the river, and the distinct wheel-marks of five guns were made out, besides those of a smaller carriage. Getting under weigh again at daylight the next morning, the ruined mosque of Imaum Subbeh was reached early in the afternoon; and the steamer running alongside the bank, a few officers landed to explore, again finding the marks of the enemy's halting-ground. The five guns had been parked near the ruin, which stood close to the waterside, and the Shah-zadeh himself had evidently occupied the little shelter afforded by the few date-trees in its immediate neighbourhood. The wheel-marks of the small carriage were again made out, and, judging from the freshness of the impressions in the clay and other appearances, not more than twenty-four hours could have elapsed since the retreating army had passed. Several fresh-made graves also gave evidence that they had buried their dead by the way; and, from the absence of the usual scraps of food around the bivouac fires, and similar indications at the picketing-places, they were evidently pressed for both provisions and forage.

We soon got under weigh again; but the river beginning to wind at very sharp angles, and decreasing in breadth at many of its bends, causing increase in proportion in the current, the remainder of the day's progress was slow; but every hope was entertained of heading the enemy before he could reach Akwâz.

The expedition brought to for the night abreast of the Arab village of Ismaini, where information was obtained from the inhabitants of the enemy having been seen passing on the previous day, with seven regiments, two thousand horse, and four guns; they had another, with its carriage broken, in a boat, which they towed up the river bank with them. With the earliest light on the 31st, the flotilla was again under weigh, and the *Comet*, now casting off the *Assyria*, proceeded alone at full power, to overtake, if possible, the boat with the gun. About nine in the morning, the first straggler from the enemy's rear-guard was seen and secured. He was starving, and in too miserable a condition to be able to give any information; but it was ascertained from some Arabs on the river-bank that the enemy had buried Agha Jhan Khan, surteep, two days previously, at Imaum Subbeh, where he had died of his wounds. Newly-made graves were also discovered here, and the fresh pug of a lion on the clay by the water's brink. About three o'clock that afternoon the Arab encampment of Omeira was reached, about fourteen miles below Akwâz, and the mortifying information received that the enemy had reached the town the previous day, and that the boat we were in pursuit of had got up with them. This news damped the spirits of all; and it being too late in the afternoon to approach the enemy's position closer, with the object of effecting anything, a halt was called for the remainder of the day, and a reconnaissance determined upon for next morning. The *Planet* and *Assyria* came up to the *Comet* before evening, and every precaution was adopted to secure the vessels against surprise during the night.

At early dawn on the 1st of April the three steamers proceeded together towards Akwâz; on nearing which, the Persian army was descried in force, but on the right bank of the river, the town standing on the left. They had a most formidable cavalry force, certainly over two thousand ; four large masses of infantry were partly screened by a low range of sand-hills, which ran along their front; and three guns were distinctly seen in position near a small mosque in their centre, a fourth being on a slope below and to the left of it. Their line fronted down the river, and at a slight angle to it, their left resting immediately upon its bank. Our small fleet steamed slowly up to within three thousand yards of the position, all busied either in surveying the river, reconnoitring the force in front, or observing the patrols of cavalry which were now riding within rifle-shot abreast of us, and watching our movements. A boat beneath the left bank for some minutes escaped with very casual notice; but suspicions being roused, it was determined to examine her. A cutter from the *Comet*, taking two officers of the party and a corporal's guard of the Highlanders, accordingly boarded her (the crew jumping overboard as the cutter approached), when she proved to be the much-coveted prize, a splendid 12-pounder brass gun being found in her. While hoisting this on board the *Comet*, a couple of horsemen approaching closer to see what we were doing, a shot was fired at them from one of Colonel Jacob's new rifles. The effect of this was most ridiculous: though not striking either. They both turned at once, galloping back at speed to the picket of some thirty cavalry which they had come from, and which also withdrew to a more respectful distance.

Some Arabs next hailed us from the shore, one was brought on board, and it was ascertained that the garrison of Akwâz did not exceed five hundred infantry and thirty horse, left to protect the stores, which had scarcely been touched by the enemy before our approach. The information appearing reliable, it was determined at once to attempt reaching the town by landing on the left bank, and circling clear of cannon-range to its east face; when, should it be found defended in much greater force, a simple reconnaissance was to be made, and an orderly return to the boats; but if practicable, the town was to be carried, and the stores burnt,—sheltering the men as much as possible from fire of the guns across the river; to draw off whose attention also, a gunboat was to ascend the river as far as prudent, and open with its two howitzers. This boat would also be of great service were the troops pressed in their return. The enemy having but two small boats on their side in which to send over any fresh men to assist those in the town, the operation, though hazardous, was perfectly feasible.

At ten o'clock the landing took place, and in a very few minutes the troops were formed, and on the move towards the town,—the gunboat also going up under sail to within easy range of the enemy's battery, and at once opening a fire of shell, coolly and ably directed by the young officer in charge of her (Mr. Hewett, mate, of the Indian navy). To magnify appearances, three separate detachments were formed, and "in rank entire," were to *act* and try to *look* like regiments in brigade; and, as the landing had taken place and these arrangements were made in jungle sufficiently high to conceal the men, it was almost impossible for the enemy to form any correct estimate of the numbers. A single line of skirmishers, each man ten or twelve paces apart, first issued from the bushes on the plain, in view of the enemy; the supports followed these, at about one hundred yards' interval, also in single rank, and with files very much loosened. At another interval of about one hundred yards, the three main detachments advanced, about two hundred yards apart, each in columns of threes, and opened out to very wide intervals.

The light company of the Highlanders was on the left, and on entering the town had to turn to the left, and, getting under cover at the water's edge, to endeavour to keep down the fire. Captain Goode's grenadiers of the 64th were in the centre, and were to move on the body of the town, and at once begin destroying the stores. Captain McAndrew's detachment on the right, composed partly of Highlanders and partly of men of the 64th, was to turn to the right on entering, and, watching any troops that might attempt the upper face of the town, also destroy whatever magazines or stores fell in its way. Complete success attended the attempt. Cowed by his recent defeat, and the heavy shells from the gunboat bringing unpleasant reminiscences of the shot at Mohammerah, the Shah-zadeh made up his mind to decamp at once, and leave his supplies to their fate. The town was undefended, the garrison going off up the river on the first appearance of the red-jackets; and on the detachments approaching, the sheik, with a retinue, came out some hundred yards to claim protection, and made his submission to the political agent, who was present with the officer in command. Every protection was immediately assured to him, and, on the understanding that he was to point out and assist in destroying the Persian magazines, it was agreed that private houses should not be searched, and the town property should be respected. The Persian army being still in position, working parties only were told off, and the remainder of the detachments placed under what cover was most available from the guns, which, most unaccountably, had not yet opened upon the town, although not five hundred yards from it,—or on the gunboat, which had now been shelling them for upwards of an hour.

A great stir was visible in the Persian lines about noon, when a fortunate shell pitching close to the small mosque where the Shah-zadeh had his head-quarters, a decided movement in retreat became visible, and a most exciting, as well as, under the circumstances, a most extraordinary, spectacle it was—an army of nine or ten thousand men, and in perfect order, retiring before three hundred. Yet so it was! Evidently mistaking us for Outram's advance-guard, and dreading to be forced to a general action, the Persian commander preferred the risk of losing his men from starvation by the road-side, on another march of one hundred miles, to Shuster (his nearest depôt of provisions), to fighting a force not half his strength, the mere appearance of a small detachment from which was sufficient to frighten him disgracefully from a formidable military position, and the whole stores of a starving army. Their infantry, still keeping in four distinct masses, went off first, marching very rapidly on a course parallel to the river, taking the four guns seen in position with them; and they were also said to have had three others of lighter metal. A small green palanquin carriage, with glass windows, and a "takh-teraidan," or mule-litter, in which Persian women of rank usually travel, were conspicuous in the midst of a strong escort. This was the carriage the tracks of which had been found at their several bivouacs. The cavalry brought up the rear, and a magnificent appearance this great body of horse presented. They certainly exceeded two thousand in number, appeared well mounted, and were dressed in long blue frocks, with trousers of lighter colour, a white belt, and the high black lambskin cap peculiar to the Persians. A sabre and long matchlock slung across their backs appeared to be their only arms, as (unusual with Asiatics) no lances were visible among them. The pick of the Bactdyari tribes, reputed the shah's best cavalry, were present among the number. They carried three standards with them, but in crimson cases, not flying. One of these horsemen remained concealed behind a wall until their whole army had proceeded about a mile, then suddenly starting from his hiding-place, he fired his matchlock at the town, as if in defiance, and galloped off at speed after his comrades. This was the last man seen of the Persian army.

Before their rear-guard had advanced many hundred yards out of their lines, the gunboat crossed, taking Captain Wray, Lord Schomberg Kerr, and Captain Green, with twenty of the Highlanders, and with utter impunity exploded a quantity of ammunition deserted by them; although—a few minutes after this took place, and when the party might easily have been cut off from the boat, had a few of their horsemen possessed the courage to dash back—they unlimbered a light gun and sent a shot at some Arab marauders who had swum the river and commenced plundering the lines they had abandoned. The town had been entered about half an hour before mid-day, and it was about two o'clock when the last of the enemy was seen. During the whole of this time the work of destroying the stores had been going on, Major Kemball first compelling the Arab inhabitants to carry down to the steamers as much of the captured flour and wheat as stowage could be found for; then, as payment for their labour, threw open to them the remainder of the immense stores of grain collected for the runaway army. The scramble which ensued must be left to imagination,—it cannot be adequately described. A sack of corn to an Arab is a prize of value: they drew knives on each other, big men knocked down little ones who had bigger bundles than their own, and at last created so serious a riot, that it was necessary to post strong guards over the stores to see the contents taken peaceably away; a singular duty indeed, considering the errand the troops had come upon, and the expectation entertained but a couple of hours previously of having to perform it with a storm of shot and shell falling around them. The appearance of the men seemed to astonish the Arabs very much; the great stature of the 64th imposing as much respectful awe as the kilts and bare knees of the Highlanders created amusement, especially among their fair sex. The latter, however, seemed fully to appreciate the good nature shown to them, in the general scramble, by our men, who might be seen helping them to fill their bundles and escape with them, without which the weaker sex would have fared but badly, as their lords and masters showed no gallantry.

Besides the immense quantity of grain thus carried off and scattered by us, fifteen cases of perfectly new firelocks and bayonets were taken, fifty-six fine mules in capital condition, a handsome horse of the Shah-zadeh's, a number of new pack-saddles, with their appointments, and a great many new intrenching-tools of different descriptions. The whole of these were brought away in the boats. The firelocks captured were of English manufacture, and had the Tower mark upon them. A large flock of sheep was also among the prizes. Of these, as many were brought off as the boats could hold, and the troops and seamen consumed many more during the stay which it was now decided to make at Akwâz, both for the moral effect and for political reasons: the remainder of the flock was presented to the sheik of the town on the depar-

G. H. H. Del. — T. Picken, Lith. George Routledge & Co. London & New York. Day & Son, Lithrs to the Queen.

AHWAS, ON THE KAROON.

ture of the expedition. The town of Akwâz is nothing beyond the usual collection of miserable hovels, constructed of mud and stone, grouped together without attempt at regularity of street or thoroughfare, and, as is peculiar to the East, where it is most imperatively necessary, utterly without drainage or provision for cleanliness or ventilation. It may contain from fifteen hundred to two thousand inhabitants, all Arabs, and a good-looking race, scarcely darker than Spaniards. There is some trifling cultivation, and a few scatterred date-trees around it, and a very pretty wooded island directly opposite, in mid-stream. Ledges of rock here impede the navigation of the river, and a few hundred yards below the town, a regular reef, called the Bund, stretches from bank to bank, with few intervals, causing dangerous rapids. Here boats coming up the Karoon have to discharge their cargoes, and place them in others which come from Shuster to meet them. This circumstance gave origin to the town. On the Bund are the ruined remains of a very ancient bridge which once spanned the rapids between the shelves of rock: a few small arches still remaining are of very singular construction, the bricks used being exceedingly small and hard, and shining like porcelain. Tradition dates this back to Alexander the Great.

The rapids once passed, the navigation of the river is unimpeded, and with moderately deep water up to Shuster, a city of considerable importance. A survey of the Karoon from this point to Mohammerah was made some years back by Commander (then Lieutenant) Selby, Indian navy, and now proved most accurate; a reconnoitring survey by Captains Wray and Green, made coming up, agreeing with it in every particular. Captain Selby, being present in command of the *Comet* and the flotilla on the river, had the gratification of finding his former scientific labour now of such great public service. The expedition remained at Akwâz during the 2nd and 3rd of April, the sheiks of the neighbouring tribes coming in readily to meet the political agent, and expressing the greatest friendship, as is usual with them to any power that may for the moment be the strongest.

The weather had all along been fine, with occasional showers, which, cooling the air, made it the more enjoyable, the thermometer not having exceeded eighty degrees since starting. Of a clear morning, the snowy range of the Bactdyari mountains was plainly visible, and the angular ridges, just tinged with the early sunlight, formed a beautiful background to a barren-looking landscape. The base of these mountains being one hundred miles distant from Akwâz, some idea may be formed of their great elevation.

On the 4th of April the expedition returned to Mohammerah, and thus closed the operations of a most successful raid, adding another laurel to the gallant sailor who conducted it ; and the little party, both blue and red jackets, and of all arms, associated on the service (especially on the *Comet*), separated with regret, and will not readily forget the expedition up the Karoon. During its absence, all the stores and tentage required for the comfort of the army had been landed, and a large regularly-pitched camp established on the open plain, about a mile from the river, the most elevated spot to be found in the neighbourhood. The detachments of the 64th and Highlanders therefore rejoined their respective regiments under circumstances of comparative comfort to what they were enduring before their departure.

CHAPTER VIII.

Scenes and Sketches in Persia.

GREAT satisfaction was expressed by Sir James at the successful issue of the service, but the news of peace with Persia having been concluded at Paris on the 4th of March previously, arriving on the same day as the return of the expedition, damped the elation of all, and considerable disgust was felt at this abrupt termination to what had promised to prove a brilliant campaign. The news of peace was promulgated in camp, by Sir James, as soon as it was received. The following amusing translation from the *Tehran Gazette* was also sent by him to the Highlanders. It gave the Persian account of the battle of Khoosh-aub, which caused much laughter, and no little astonishment at their impudent romancing.

Both officers and men proved what adepts the Persian authorities are at romancing, and making the best of a bad case:—

"TEHRAN GOVERNMENT GAZETTE EXTRAORDINARY.

"ACCORDING to an express sent by Sooja-ool-Moolk, it appears that the English army, consisting of five regiments and ten guns, marched on the 8th Toomalee-ool-Sami (3rd February, 1857), to Char-Kota, four fursucks from Bushire, to work some injury to the army under Sooja-ool-Moolk before it could join the other Moslem troops. The Sooja-ool-Moolk, with three thousand infantry, three hundred cavalry, and twelve guns, on the 9th (4th), contemplated a night attack on the enemy. When he had proceeded four miles from Brans-jaru, the rain began to fall very heavily. The English advanced about four miles from Char-Kota, where they entered holes, and went behind irregularities of the ground. The Moslem troops, having no shelter from the rain, and finding their own encampment nearer than that of the enemy, went back, purposing to return to the battle. As the English army were under cover, they reached Brásjoon next morning. On the night of the 12th (7th), the Sooja-ool-Moolk, at the head of three thousand picked infantry and eight guns, attacked the English, whose advanced guard, becoming aware of this movement, fired a signal gun. The British, unable to remove the enormous quantity of their ammunition (owing to the rain), blew it up, and returned towards Bushire.

"The victorious Persian army pursued the English to within three and a half fursucks (fourteen miles) of Bushire, when reinforcements, consisting of two regiments, four hundred cavalry, and ten guns, came out to their relief, on which they turned back again and wanted to fight. Though the strength of the victorious Persian army did not exceed three thousand infantry and eight guns, still they heeded not the overpowering numbers of the enemy but eagerly rushed forward to the slaughter. They fought heroically for four hours, beginning at daylight; and twice breaking through the English squares, entered their lines and strove vigorously. It is also reported that General Stalker, who first arrived at Bushire, was killed in that action, but it requires confirmation.

"Among the Persian officers, Mahomed Koolee Khan, surteep, was wounded with a grape shot; and Alee Khan, surteep, of the Karagoozloo regiment, received a sword wound when he penetrated into the English ranks, but I thank God neither of them have come to harm. Owing to the intensity of the rain, each party was obliged to desist from further warfare and returned to its own camp, leaving on both sides several guns sticking in the mud. An accurate account of the killed could not be obtained, owing to the inclemency of the weather; but the killed on the side of the English must have been from seven or eight hundred to one thousand, and on the part of the Persians, from three to five hundred. The sukeseetchee-bashee, who has proceeded to the field of battle, will shortly write a true account of the affair, and, D.V., it shall be published in the next number of the *Gazette*."

"Translated by, and signed,

"J. R. L. TAYLOR,

"Captain 18th N.I.,

"Political Secretary."

From the immense amount of fiction in this, can only be gleaned the facts that they had eight guns in our front at Khoosh-aub, and that the alarm of a night attack on the evening before the march from Brásjoon, had not been entirely groundless. The mode in which they account for the grand explosion on the night we marched, by stating it to be our own powder—and for the capture of their guns by sticking "several on both sides" in the mud—is diplomacy worthy of the father of lies himself. But, grossly as they may, and notoriously do, mystify and delude the imbecile monarch who now fills the throne of the shahs—how the Persian officers may succeed in persuading him that we have not taken Mohammerah from them by open force—that we have never occupied it, nor driven the Shah-zadeh from Akwâz and destroyed his stores—still remains to be proved.

From this time all again returned to the same style of life as in camp at Bushire, even to the working parties; with the single difference that instead of constructing, they were as busy in destroying works. However, fine weather and good health made all cheerful; indeed it would be impossible to have had troops in finer working condition than the division then was, when the termination of the war approached. Thoroughly acclimatized, and inured to exposure in all weather, feet hardened for marching, and men handy at hutting themselves, as well as cooking quickly, and other little campaigning requisites only to be learned from experience—it seemed almost like wilfully destroying a beautiful machine to send troops in such order again to play at soldiers in Indian cantonments.

Matters continued very dull for several days—not even camp gossip of any kind to enliven society; and the departure of the 64th regiment to rejoin their own (first) division, at Bushire, was the only occurrence that could be noted. The *Comet* had been despatched to Bagdad by the general, immediately on hearing of peace, and her return was now anxiously awaited, as it was expected that she would bring the conditions; and a general idea prevailed that the terms granted would be found to be far too favourable, and such as the late occurrences, if known at home, would have prevented their receiving. Excursions to Bussorah, twenty-five miles distant, were now resorted to by as many as could get leave, as some relief from the tedious monotony of life in camp, and an escape from the heat under canvas, which had daily increased. The Turkish authorities were very obliging, and showed all the civility in their power to the different parties visiting the town.

The trip up the river is not interesting, as there is no view beyond the date-trees on either bank; but once arrived, the remains of this formerly populous and flourishing city amply repay the tedious inconvenience of being cramped in a boat during a six hours' pull to visit them. Bussorah once covered a very great extent of ground, and that not many years ago; but now it is little larger than Bushire, and far more ruinous. Its fortifications exist only in detached pieces, and are ridiculous as military works. The town, utterly unpaved, has no thoroughfare for wheeled vehicles—indeed such appear to be unknown: the streets are so narrow as scarcely to admit of half a dozen passers at the same moment, and after a shower are almost impracticable from mud. The ruin of the whole city is accounted for by its having (even within late years) been twice depopulated—once by plague in 1838, and again by cholera in 1845. The only object of particular interest which it possesses is the bazaar, which reminds one far more of descriptions in the "Arabian Nights" than even that at Cairo. It is low, and with a very singular arched roof. There are stalls on either side, each touching its neighbour, and displaying either gaudy silk and woollen goods, or arms, pipe-sticks, Arab chogees (cloaks), slippers of every dye; and grocery and tobacco-shops, interrupted here and there by coffee divans, crowded by idlers smoking and gossiping, which may be seriously included among the graver necessities of Asiatic life, and with both sexes—the women going to the hummums (or baths), and the men to the divans. Whether this same remark may not, with equal truth, be made of our own countrymen and women sojourning in the East, I leave those who have had any experience of Indian cantonment life to say. To return to Bussorah, a motley throng crowded its narrow causeway; wild-looking Bedouins from the desert, with their glittering, almost snake-like, eyes; gaudily dressed, baggy-breeched, Bashi-bazouks, with waistbands full of "impossible" pistols; sedate-looking Armenians; Arabs of the city, in their singularly picturesque costume; women shuffling about—not walking—in yellow Wellingtons, swathed, like mummies, in blue calico, and showing the tips of two fingers and one eye; and here and there a Turkish officer, in tight European frock and trowsers, contrasting sadly with the scarlet fez; all combining to form a picture sufficiently interesting from its novelty to make amends even for the punishment to the olfactory nerves which imagination must supply, for description fails.

The recent events at Mohammerah procured for the British visitors in the bazaar considerable respect as well as attention; the conquerors of works before which their own arms in their last attempt failed (Mohammerah having always been a bone of contention in their quarrels with the shah), could not be treated with Moslem insolence; and consequently salaams and obeisances were as plentifully bestowed now as the epithets "kafir," "infidel," "unclean dog," "son of a burnt father," would have been, but a short time previously, in the same place and by the very same people. The great number of blind to be met excited general remark, as nearly one third of the inhabitants appeared to be suffering from either total blindness or the loss of one eye. With the exception of the Armenians, the male population go armed to the teeth; and such is the insecurity of property and inefficiency of their police (who levy black-mail upon, instead of protecting the inhabitants), that by four o'clock in the afternoon the shops in the bazaar are all closed, and the large gates at either end shut at dark. Whatever the people of Bussorah may have sacrificed in politeness, they amply atoned to themselves for by avarice and extortion. Every article in demand suddenly rose at least two hundred per cent. Tobacco and rose-water never before brought such prices; and poultry, butter, eggs, *cum multis aliis* of the minor articles, drove an equally thriving trade with the more costly produce of the bazaar.

Bussorah stands on a creek, or rather canal, about one mile and a half distant from the Euphrates, and still possesses an extensive commerce. The banks of the creek are fringed with foliage, among which the European eye rests with pleasure on the walnut, apple, mulberry, apricot, and vine—familiar even amid their Oriental associates—and which, thus suddenly recognized, seemed, rapid as was the glance bestowed upon them, to have home and its reminiscences stamped upon every leaf. The Persian embassy, one of the best houses in the place, abuts on the creek, and had but a few days previously been illuminated for the victory (?) they claimed to have won at Khoosh-aub. Perhaps the unfortunate fact that the unclean kafirs were then in actual possession of their stronghold, prevented a similar display for another victory at Mohammerah. Be that as it may, the usually crowded windows and couches on the balcony of the embassy were invariably deserted on the appearance of a red uniform, which were now frequent in the town. A small fort, with some very ancient and unserviceable guns, guards the entrance of the creek from the Euphrates, where a corvette and sloop are also generally at anchor, and are ample defence against their cowardly neighbours. The commodore commanding these vessels was particularly polite to his English visitors, hoisting the British ensign and firing six guns when a party of officers quitted his ship.

A pasha, with his head-quarters at Bussorah, governs the town and district, the revenue of which he farms from the government, a measure which of itself puts at once all hope of improvement to the condition of either the town or people out of the question. The imperial treasury exacting from the pasha the highest possible rent, and granting to him but a very uncertain tenure of office—self-interest at once steps in, and impels him to extort to the last kraun (shilling) from the merchants in taxes, and the Arab tribes in tribute-money—all that he can scrape together—leaving him to his own resources entirely to collect this, and for which he not unfrequently has to fight. The only troops in Bussorah were some Bashi-bazouk cavalry and a few infantry irregulars, who receive about the same pay as the sepoy troops in India, but at very uncertain periods. One of their number, who had served under British colours formerly, in the Punjab irregulars, entering into conversation with an officer, told him that he thought his present service best, as he made more, and had no work, no guards, no parades, &c., &c.; but, judging from appearances, these fellows were worth about as much as soldiers as their neighbours across the river. In such a state of things, roads, public buildings, or extension of commerce, are impossible, and it may safely be foreboded that, under Turkish control, managed as at present, few years will elapse before Bussorah, once the emporium of Asiatic Turkey, will be among the things that were.

Meanwhile, nothing but the usual routine took place at Mohammerah, though one occurrence certainly deserves notice. Some few days after the conclusion of peace had been made known, the Shah-zadeh, who had been informed of it from Tehran, not feeling very comfortable as to what General Outram's intentions might still be pending the ratification of the treaty, sent in a messenger to him, to inquire whether he was aware of the satisfactory issue of the negotiations. Sir James's curt and soldierly reply to the question was—that, had he not been aware of it, he should have been at Shuster to beat his quarters up days before. This answer may have quieted the Persian prince's apprehensions, but certainly could not have flattered his vanity; and, plain speaking being a thing unknown at a Persian court, most probably astonished him a little.

The intelligence brought to us some days before was now also fully confirmed, and the enemy's army described to be in such extremity, from want of provisions, that they might at any moment be heard of as having dispersed and each man seeking to subsist as best he might,—the silence of their guns, and non-resistance to our proceedings at Akwâz, being fully accounted for by the fact of their having but seven mule-loads of ammunition with their entire army; and as they were expecting, when they moved off, that they might possibly be overtaken and brought to action, they would, in case they had expended this upon us, have been almost without the means of resistance.

To insure this army fighting to the last, the shah had actually ordered the hill tribes to close the passes against them, leaving them no retreat; so that five hundred sabres would in this instance have secured us the Shah-zadeh himself, his guns, and his army, days before the intelligence reached us which tied the general's hands.

Nelson is once said to have exclaimed,—"Were I to die now, 'want of frigates' would be found stamped upon my heart." In the present instance, Sir James might well have repeated his great predecessor's words; but his frigates would have been cavalry, an arm which, singular to say, every British force that has yet taken the field, has, without exception, been deficient in—although no country in the world can match the troopers which Great Britain possesses. Our regulars and irregulars, Asiatic as well as European, are undoubtedly the first of their description. The Cossack cavalry of Russia has nothing to place beside the Scinde horse—and Balaklava will long tell its own tale for the dragoons of England. The greater mismanagement, as well as pity, is it, then, that this magnificent arm should never be in sufficient force when results almost incalculable might, as on this occasion, have been secured by their presence.

The duties in camp being comparatively light, and the presence of many of the officers not actually necessary, more prolonged leave of absence was allowed by Sir James than that required for a simple visit to Bussorah; and the steamers taking despatches affording opportunities of seeing Bagdad, the trip was eagerly sought after, and leave taken advantage of. The *Planet* steamer accordingly left Mohammerah on the morning of the 29th of April, with despatches for our ambassador, in expectation of bringing back the ratification of the treaty to Sir James, and a very agreeable party was arranged to proceed in her. Leaving the camp at daylight, the voyage up the river commenced, and a short halt was made at the British residency at Maryhill about noon. This is the head-quarters of Mr. Taylor, the British consul, whose residence in such a locality through every month of the year is assuredly little to be envied. The house is a building of some pretension on the river-bank, enclosed within a walled courtyard. A monument recording the fate of the unfortunate men drowned in Colonel Chesney's expedition is erected against one of its walls; a large Arab village is on its lower face, and a deep date grove backs the whole. Some very interesting sculptures from Nineveh were lying on the wharf, awaiting embarkation for England, which, with the quaint epitaphs marking the rude graves of one or two seamen in this far away spot, were all to attract attention.

From Maryhill to Korna, where the Tigris joins the Euphrates, the latter river presented nothing new; but at the junction of these two magnificent streams, which for some distance are clearly discernible from each other (the waters of the Euphrates being much the clearest), a striking change takes place in the character of the scenery. Korna itself is an insignificant village, remarkable for nothing beyond its important and picturesque situation. Entering the Tigris, the belt of date-trees almost immediately terminates; patches of cultivation show themselves more frequently, and the country (though still a dead level) has a fertile and less desert look.

The increased number of the Arab tribes, their larger encampments, as well as the immense flocks and herds, and beauty of the horses frequently seen with them, at once drew attention. The value of these latter is right well known by their owners, horses of good caste being very high priced, even as two year olds, and the mares (if of any noted stock) actually unobtainable. Excepting foals, all were kept perfectly swathed in thick clothing, even out at pasture; and the best shelter of their rude tents or huts, as well as the best of their food, were evidently the established right of the pet mare of the family. The country on the banks of the Tigris differs much from that of the Karoon and Euphrates—it has the willow, poplar, and cypress jungle of the former skirting its immediate bank, but instead of desert beyond, it is for the most part green, beautiful pasturage, with but few tracts of entirely barren land. This, of course, accounts for the increased population and their better appearance.

These Arab tribes are a wild-looking but well-favoured and muscular race, of middle stature, dark brown in colour, with well-shaped features, and though professional robbers whenever they have it in their power, are excessively cautious where attack might be dangerous, for they are cowardly and treacherous in the extreme. The 24-pounders of the *Planet* gained her not only civility but respect. From time immemorial these tribes have levied black-mail upon every boat or traveller passing within their limits, and our flag has actually submitted to the same insulting impost (on the native conciliation system), when one well-inflicted punishment would at once have stopped it. The commissariat supplies for the camp at Mohammerah were actually seized by these marauders a few days before our departure, and the officers and others in charge of them obliged to flee for their lives—and yet, owing to missionary influence at head-quarters, this gross offence was passed over, and the tribute demanded actually paid in money instead of grape-shot; these savages of course imagining that they had awed us into submission.

Should it ever be intended to open up the commerce attainable by the splendid rivers of these regions, now better known to the public, the ill-timed concession—at a moment when we were in a position to enforce respect to our flag—will but ensure violence and bloodshed when means will be wanting to chastise aggressors. At the different wooding stations, however, the Arabs came readily among us, a few only being armed (chiefly with light spears and swords of rude manufacture), and brought what articles they had likely to find sale among us. Their women accompanied them in considerable numbers, many of them with no slight pretensions to good looks, which, contrary to all Eastern notions of propriety, they were by no means chary of displaying. Judging from all appearances, these tribes must lead even happier lives than more civilized people, having but few wants and those easily supplied by the means around them—the two extremes, great wealth and abject poverty, being utterly unknown.

The quantity of game seen on the river side exceeded even that on the Karoon; the duck were literally innumerable, and black partridge rose from nearly every bush; wild hog (of which some were killed swimming the river), wolves, antelopes, and jackals, were constantly in view, and both guns and rifles found constant employment — a walk of a few hundred yards, while the steamer was wooding, making no slight addition to the table for the day. The lion is also occasionally to be found in the lower lands adjacent to the Tigris.

About one hundred miles above Korna, on the right bank of the river, stands the tomb of the prophet-scribe Ezra, a pretty mosque of tesselated brickwork, surmounted by a green cupola, and enclosed within a wall also intended for defensive purposes, being crenellated for musketry; it is picturesquely situated at a bend of the river, and, being still held in great odour of sanctity, is kept in good repair. The surrounding tribes bring their dead from great distances for interment in its immediate neighbourhood. On the 4th of May Kootul-Humaru was reached, where is a small Arab fort in good condition, intended only as a defence against the tribes armed with matchlocks, the walls being of mud, and barely more than bullet-proof. The Turks have a small party of Bashi-bazouks stationed here, who were busy putting the place in order, having turned the Arabs out of it only a few days previously to our arrival, after a trifling skirmish, as usual, on account of the tribute. A larger body of these irregulars had been met with in a fleet of canoes lower down the river, and the curiosity as well as surprise which their appearance had occasioned, was now fully satisfied, on finding that they were on the same errand as their comrades at Kootul-Humaru. These latter pretended to be indignant, forsooth, at our having inspected their fortification! Nothing new presented itself in the character of the country during the progress of the next day or two, excepting the appearance of a high mountain range in the extreme distance. The same dead level of rich pasture land prevailed, and the population on the banks continued numerous, and game of all kinds abundant. The mountain snows rapidly filling the river, also delayed our advance, and the passage was becoming somewhat tedious and monotonous, when, on the afternoon of the 6th of May, a most singular phenomenon occurred, which revived the flagging interest.

The day had been cloudy throughout, but about three o'clock the horizon darkened, and what were at first imagined to be heavy banks of clouds collecting for a thunder-storm suddenly made their appearance: these came sweeping rapidly up, but, as they approached, assumed a new and most alarming appearance, —no longer cloud, but dust and vapour mixed, and piled, roll over roll, high in the heavens, extending like a solid wall far as the eye could reach, here and there violently agitated by some fierce whirlwind. Fortunate, indeed, was it for the beholders that the *Planet* was not near its vortex, or she must assuredly have met the same fate as the unfortunate steamer of Colonel Chesney's expedition; as it happened, before the blast struck her she was secured close under the lee of what little shelter the low river-bank afforded, with an anchor down, and the awnings and everything that could catch the wind removed.

The approach of this fearful visitant would be most correctly described as awfully sublime, it advanced massively and regularly, as though one half of the earth had been bodily raised up and was hanging in mid-air to overwhelm the other—the outer edge as abrupt and clearly defined as that of some stupendous projecting cliff, and not unlike such in colour, being of a dusky brown hue; and near the ground, where the wind rolled it in eddies, huge chasms and caverns seemed formed, as though actually cut out of the solid rock. The cattle herded together and lay down, evidently terrified, as it neared them; and the birds, quitting the air, also sought refuge upon the ground.

For a few seconds before the crash broke an unearthly stillness prevailed, then a few large drops of rain and a terrific gust of wind struck the steamer, and instantly afterwards the dust-storm was on her. Daylight became suddenly and most singularly eclipsed rather than darkened, for though vision was limited to very little distance on either hand, it still was not the black obscurity which night throws around, but rather a thick, palpable veil, perfectly impervious to view, yet still admitting a dusky, subdued light. This lasted for some three or four hours, during which dust, so fine as to penetrate within the watches on board, fell thickly, attended with a sense of almost suffocation; and a fierce rushing of the wind was audible at some distance, although, after the first blast, a calm prevailed near the steamer. Had all the cannon in the universe been discharged at the same instant—the uproar, smoke, and dust from ever so mighty a battery would have made but a feeble comparison with the grand spectacle that was displayed before us. It was, in truth, terrifically grand, and imposed a feeling of awe upon us—helpless as all human means would have been, if involved in its resistless vortex, and ignorant as we were of what fearful consequences might be concealed within its impenetrable depths. All, however, passed over without accident, though considerable time elapsed before sufficient light returned to enable us to continue our course; and the day closed with a lovely, cool, star-lit evening.

During our progress on the 7th, the only objects of fresh interest were some very ancient ruins on the right bank, called "the tombs of the lover and his betrothed," to which Arab tradition attaches one of the usual tales of romance, bloodshed, and early death appropriate to such a title, of which the weather-beaten walls before us were now the sole memento. It was to be remarked, though, that the lover's tomb could boast of a roof,

G.H.H. Del. — T Picken, Lith. George Routledge & Co. London & New York. Day & Son, Lith[rs] to the Queen.

CHOSROE'S ARCH, RUINS OF CTESIPHON.

which his betrothed's could not, a fact certainly not over creditable to posthumous Arab gallantry. Early on the 8th of May the ruins of Ctesiphon were reached, the Tigris winding so abruptly as almost to encircle them, and as considerable time was required for the steamer to make the *détour* (more particularly on account of the increased current at this spot), ample leisure was afforded for a satisfactory survey of ruins as extraordinary and interesting, both from antiquity and historical association, as any now existing. The boundary walls of this once mighty city enclosed a great area, and they are plainly discernible by the high sand-drift mounds which have for ages been collecting against and over them, extending in a radius of several miles from the left bank of the river. Considerable ruins are also observable on the opposite side, as also remains of masonry just above the city, which might almost warrant the supposition that the Tigris was once bridged at this spot, and that a large suburb of the city existed on the right bank.

In the centre of the buried as well as ruined

city, high amid the sand-covered foundations of temples, theatres, baths, gymnasia, and other countless structures of Alexander's great general, rises the arch of Chosroes, the entrance of the Parthian monarch's palace of that name, on which it is said that the sun shone more than one thousand years before our Saviour's birth. This venerable relic of the past is truly magnificent. The arch is 128 feet in height, and of great span, extending the full depth of the building, but it has fallen in in many places within. The outer face is, however, nearly perfect. The wings on either side are each some 250 feet in length. They are divided into four or five stories of alternate pilasters and small arches nearly elliptical, and what is the most extraordinary feature of the whole building, there is not a single perpendicular in it,—all the lines, even to the sides of the great arch, bearing inwards to each other. The bricks of which it is composed are as hard as granite, and with a surface nearly as polished as porcelain: they are about a foot square in size, and three inches thick. The Turks (barbarians as they are), wanting the materials for building at Bagdad, tried to throw the arch down by digging into its base; but, finding the labour too severe and not likely to repay the cost, after disfiguring it along the whole front, desisted. On entering the ruin, a large flock of wild duck started from the niches and upper ledges of the masonry, making the old walls echo with the sharp quick flapping of their wings, and took their way to the neighbouring marshes. As a fact pendant to finding wild duck in such a singular locality, it may be here mentioned that they were constantly seen to perch on trees and bushes and on walls during the voyage up.

Close to Chosroes's palace stands a small mosque in good repair, said to cover the tomb of the prophet's *barber;* a spot held in such sanctity that infidel presence was not permitted to sully it by inspection. A few palm trees, the only ones for some distance, are planted round it. Save this tomb and the noble arched ruin, all that now marks the site of the great Grecian soldier's city are the sand-mounds covering its widely spread foundations.

Fame and name alone, and a barber's tomb, are all that time has left unscathed of Ctesiphon.

On the right bank of the river, some half-mile above the ruins, the Turks have established a gunpowder manufactory for their arsenal at Bagdad, which is only some forty miles distant. The approach to it, now commencing, is picturesque in the extreme, the river gradually widening, and foliage becoming more frequent on its banks. The Tigris is in truth a noble stream, with an average depth of from twenty to twenty-five feet; and the fact of so large a river increasing both its breadth and depth so many miles above its junction with another, and as it nears its own source, is exceedingly singular. The dead level of the country, however, many miles of which are under water during the season of the inundations, fully accounts for the expenditure of the vast volumes of water before reaching their narrowed outlet at Korna.

Melancholy indeed is it that a portion of the richest country in the world, blessed with an almost heavenly climate for eight months of the year, should be untilled in the hands of vagabond tribes, when nothing but a little of man's industry is required to change it into a veritable paradise,—the original garden of our first parents before their fall being actually fixed by Arab tradition in the immediate neighbourhood of Korna, on the delta of the Tigris and Euphrates.

CHAPTER IX.

A Visit to Bagdad, and the Voyage back.

When within some four or five miles of Bagdad, country houses with gardens (at this time in most blooming condition) and orchards of European fruit trees thickly line the water's side, until turning a sudden bend of the river, the city of the Kaliphs bursts at once upon the view. Bright coloured mosques and minarets, with green and golden cupolas; quaint looking houses with suspicious balconies, from which to eject sacked ladies into the foaming Tigris; frowning batteries and fortifications, much requiring visits from bricklayers and labourers; trees, flags, basket boats, women like bundles, with long black shawls tied across half their faces; fruit sellers, water carriers, and grave looking Turks of all sorts, seem, as it were, to seize upon the attention at one and the same moment, until, glancing up the stream near the serail, the pasha's residence, the eye is fairly arrested by the singular bridge of boats spanning the rushing river, here about seven hundred yards wide, and with a current of some five knots an hour. The *Planet* dropped her anchor close to the British consulate, a large commodious house, with a pretty garden in front abutting on the river. Here a most hospitable reception awaited us; and, having despatched a messenger to the pasha to ascertain when it would be convenient for him to receive a visit from us, the remainder of the afternoon was passed in a ramble through the bazaars. Haroun Alraschid may well have had endless romantic adventures during his *incognito* night walks through these; for the narrow arched alleys and mysterious doorways leading from the crowded thoroughfares almost seem constructed for no purpose save waylaying some princess of fabulous beauty, or for gloomy conspirators to whisper treason in.

The bazaar covers a great extent of ground, one long street extending through the centre, with others crossing it at right angles, each street being appropriated by one particular trade, and all alike narrow, unpaved, and dirty, with the additional nuisance of being infested by innumerable mangy dogs. Coffee divans, crowded with half-stupified smokers, are at every corner, where professional story-tellers still follow their calling, as in the time of the charming Scheherazade and the "Thousand and One Nights." A far superior class of people to those at Bussorah are here to be met with. Wealthy Turks on superb horses, with retinues of eight or ten slaves equally well mounted—and highly-adorned mule litters with their fair inmates perfectly veiled, or coquettishly allowing a slip of the *yasmak*, which happened more than once during the stroll of the Feringhee party—were passing frequently. As it was the Ramazan, during which a strict fast is kept from dawn until sunset and no business transacted, the pasha fixed nine o'clock in the evening for receiving our visit; and shortly before that hour, an escort of furashees, some of them carrying long paper lanterns, arrived at the consulate to conduct us. Our way lay through the main bazaar, in which no trifling

G. H. H. del. — E. Walker, lith. George Routledge & C° London & New-York. Day & Son, Lith[rs] to the Queen

BAGDAD

commotion was created by the appearance of a bevy of British uniforms at that hour. The pasha's residence is a large quadrangular barrack-like building, of which the centre is occupied by himself, the wings by his retainers, whose name appeared to be legion. A guard was drawn up at the entrance for our reception. Ascending a long flight of steps, which led to a spacious hall, the pasha met us at the doorway and conducted us to a row of ottomans extending across the further end, his own suite and the officers of the garrison lining the sides of the apartment. After a separate introduction to him by the senior of our party, coffee and pipes were introduced, and conversation became general. Of middle stature, with expressive sensible countenance and most prepossessing address, the pasha is said to possess considerable ability. His pashalik being of the first class, constitutes him one of the dignitaries of the empire, and his manners were eminently those of a man perfectly conscious of his own importance. Speaking French and Italian fluently, he was frank and unreserved in replying to our inquiries, and giving information as well regarding his province as the town and its immediate neighbourhood. He had a *corps d'armée* of thirty thousand men under his own immediate command, distributed over the pashalik, of which, six thousand infantry and artillery were then present with his headquarters in Bagdad; about three thousand cavalry and the horses of his batteries were, he informed us, at some seven or eight miles' distance in the country, on account of forage failing in the town.

After our visit had extended over half an hour, iced sherbet was handed round, and we took our leave, returning to our quarters attended by the same escort and lanterns as before. The following morning was devoted to visiting the fortifications and barracks, and a stroll across the bridge of boats to the opposite quarter of the city. The works are in bad condition, and fast crumbling to decay, but they are of good profile and well-placed, and, at no very great expense or trouble, might be restored. Many of the guns on the ramparts are most singular, some of them old Venetian pieces (stamped with the winged lion) of two centuries back; others Persian, and many Russian, also of great age. The barracks are fine buildings, but kept in the most filthy condition, and, from the number of cats prowling about them, an extraordinary predilection for the feline race must prevail among the Turkish soldiery. These last appeared cleanly enough in their white undress, and well cared for; many of them, especially among the artillery, wore the Silistrian medal, which they stepped forward to show us with no little pride. They paid most marked respect wherever they met us, and their sentries invariably saluted on our passing their posts, although not in uniform.

At the entrance of the artillery barrack is a trophy gun of immense length and calibre, Persian, and of far larger bore than our 68-pounders, cast of brass. It bears traces of very rough service, having the dents of two large shot marks on the chase and breech, and is also split at the muzzle, and the vent much run. The age and weight of the gun could not be ascertained. Thirty field-guns, 9 and 12-pounders, among which were some howitzers, and all in most serviceable order, occupied the gun-sheds attached to this barrack; and the arsenal, which they also allowed us to inspect, appeared well-stored and kept with considerable system. Crossing the bridge of boats, the opposite quarter of Bagdad did not repay the visit, as among all the foul and dirty places of either "Christendom or Paynim far countrie," that suburb decidedly holds a pre-eminence marked in more senses than one. The view of the main city from that side is, however, very striking and beautiful, and the great mosque shows to particular advantage. This structure though, our Moslem friends carefully explained to us, was not to be even approached by unbelievers at that holy season, and never can be entered by them; so our curiosity, though not a little excited by viewing its superb dome of green and gold, and its graceful minarets, had perforce to remain unsatisfied. The boat-bridge is of very simple construction, the boats being moored singly, head to stream, and connected with each other by chains and planks. Mules and horses cross it readily, but no wheel-vehicle ever attempts it. A walk across gives the best idea of the force of the stream, which rushes between the boats with the velocity of a mill-race.

Passing the pasha's stables on our return, we entered them, and well were they worth the visit. Large airy buildings erected round a square next to the seraglio, and kept as clean and scrupulously tidy as the barracks were disgracefully dirty. Long troughs extending along the front of each building, over which brass cocks were let into the wall, communicating with pipes bringing water from the river, supplied that necessary in unlimited quantity, and contributed much to the general cleanliness. The stabling would hold about four hundred horses, but a small portion only of the pasha's stud was then in Bagdad, the remainder being with his cavalry camp: still there were many very handsome animals present, and a few beautiful mares with foals at their sides. Ascending a very ancient minaret close to the palace, the view of the city is exceedingly striking, and far more oriental than either Cairo or Constantinople. This, however, the almost total absence of European costume would alone account for; the *attachés* to the political officers, and to the depôt for the small naval establishment on the river, with one single enterprising merchant, comprising the whole Frank society in Bagdad.

The naval depôt is close to the consulate, and near it reside the wives of the seamen of the flotilla. These are Armenian Christians, and speak no English, and as Turkish or Arabic are acquirements made by Jack usually after marriage, the courtship must open under, to say the least, difficulties. Notwithstanding this, nearly all the seamen of the *Comet* steamer have married here. One of them, endeavouring to explain the matter, said that "first one of them got a wife, and then the rest got introduced to her relations, and they soon knowed enough of the country language to get on comfortable."

Among the upper classes of the Armenians, many very beautiful faces may be seen in the balconies, and peeping through the latticed windows overhanging the streets and river. They are a fair race, brown hair and blue eyes being as frequently met with amongst them as the darker colours; but the features and expression are decidedly Asiatic, and the dress adopted both by the men and women is exceedingly picturesque and becoming. Although Christians, the women go veiled when out of doors, though probably more to avoid insult from the Moslem population, than from any idea that propriety required it.

The fruit season having just commenced, in the early morning the market, rich in tempting-looking basket loads, and gay with bright flowers, presented a treat indeed to English eyes. It was not a little amusing, also, to watch the veiled beauties making little opportunities for affording a glimpse of occasionally a very pretty face, while chaffering among apples, grapes, mulberries, and apricots, which appeared strange, and filberts and honest red-faced hazel-nuts actually seemed to have no business there among turbans, yellow slippers, and sack-jumping young ladies—for such, be it said with sorrow, is the graceful action of the Turkish dames, in the streets at least; and whose charms, could one but get a fair look at them, would doubtless as little bear comparison with those of our own fair maids as the flowers and fruit with their English namesakes.

The hummums are numerous, and nearly always crowded. At any of these, the luxury (*query* infliction) of being steamed, suffocated, scraped, lathered, scalded, beaten, jumped upon, dashed into a state of syncope with icy water, and then left in a most favourable condition for catching cold, may be enjoyed at very moderate expense, save of constitution, at any hour of the day. Some of these establishments were very luxuriously fitted up, and the number of listless, effeminate-looking men, smoking and dozing for hours on the ottomans —as though such were the only business of their lives—too faithfully told the tale of a declining, feeble, and worthless race.

The crescent that once menaced Europe, is a waning moon indeed now; though half the world will be shaken by another bloody war—in all probability—before nations decide what standard shall replace it.

Despatches having arrived from England, with which we were to return to camp, our stay at Bagdad drew to a close, leaving a conviction that, although well worth a visit, without society to compensate, and with stag-hunting alone for out-of-door amusement—even though the best of that is to be had, game always to be found, and good horses to follow it—still, for a lengthened residence, the city of the Kaliphs must be dull indeed, and during the hot months, anything but a spot to be desired. The ruins of Nineveh were but eighty miles distant, and great disappointment was felt at being unable to visit them; but time was wanting, and ourselves under military control, even during our holiday. We had, therefore, to leave our hospitable entertainers at the consulate with the best grace we might, and return to Mohammerah, aided by assistance as mighty as that of Bagdad's genii of old—viz., steam.

On the 10th of May the *Planet* commenced her downward voyage, leaving our ambassador the Hon. C. A. Murray, at Bagdad, to await the arrival of the envoy from Tehran, who was to escort him on his return to the shah's court; his reception there, with all honours, being one of the articles of the treaty insisted upon, and which must be felt as most humiliating by the Persians. Many of that nation were in Bagdad during our stay; but, as at Bussorah, they carefully avoided meeting us. We were informed by our Armenian visitors, that, up to the fall of Mohammerah, they had talked very largely in the coffee divans of utterly exterminating the unclean dogs of Englishmen, and were now as proportionately twitted by the Turks at their thrashing; the latter hating the Iranees even more bitterly than Catholic hated Protestant in the early days of the Reformation. The closing events of our short but decisive campaign, although so suddenly brought to a close, will doubtless long leave after them a wholesome dread of British power among a people hitherto the most boasting and vainglorious, as perhaps contemptible, of Eastern nations. A lesson has been taught, sufficiently severe to reach the shah, even through the falsehood and chicanery of his nobles; and Russian influence has received a check from the effects of which it will require both time and very favourable opportunity to recover.

The return voyage occupied but half the time of the upward trip, and was accomplished without any fresh occurrence of interest, except passing the *Comet* steamer below Kootul-Humaru. She was taking up the two Captains Green and Dr. Wood, as a mission; who, after accompanying the embassy to Tehran, were to proceed to Herat, and witness its evacuation. Bushire remained in British hands until that and the other conditions of the treaty might be fulfilled. Mohammerah was reached on the 14th of May, when the camp was found to be breaking up, the Highlanders and Blake's horse artillery having actually sailed on their return to India, and the following field force order, by Sir James Outram, decreed the dissolution of the second division. Its career in the field was thus prematurely closed when the troops composing it had become inured to the hardships of actual service, familiar with its duties, and confident in its leader whenever opportunity might offer.

Mixed feelings prevailed in camp at the separation of regiments so long associated together. Some rejoiced at the prospect of returning to the quiet of cantonment life and its comforts, yet many regretted the close of the war before an advance on Ispahan should have afforded a field for friendly rivalry for distinction and honour, even at the price of months of hardship and a Persian summer. Still, as operations had finally closed, fortunate indeed, was it, that the troops could be removed before the commencement of the reputed deadly fever season at Mohammerah, where the thermometer already stood at one hundred and two degrees in the tents, and might be expected to range to one hundred and twenty degrees before the expiration of the ensuing three months.

"FIELD FORCE ORDER.

"Camp, Mohammerah,
"9th May, 1857.

"Consequent on the cessation of hostilities in Persia, the following troops will be held in readiness to embark for India:—

"Third troop of horse-artillery to Kurrachee; first company second battalion of artillery to Kurrachee; reserve companies to Bombay; her

Majesty's 64th regiment to Vingorla; her Majesty's 78th Highlanders to Bombay; light battalion to Bombay; Madras sappers and miners to Bombay.

"2. The 23rd Native Light Infantry and the 26th Native Infantry are transferred to the first division, and will proceed to Bushire, with the detachment of Scinde horse and Land Transport corps now at Mohammerah.

"3. The staff of the second division will return to Bombay, with the exception of the engineers, ordnance, and commissariat departments, which will proceed to Bushire and await further instructions.

"4. Brigadier-general Jacob, C.B., will command the troops stationed at Bushire, which will be organized as follows:—Cavalry brigade: 3rd regiment light cavalry, Scinde horse, Poona horse, Aden troop, 14th King's light dragoons—Brigadier Stewart. Artillery brigade: 4th troop horse artillery, 3rd light field battery, 5th light field battery, 8th light field battery, three companies of the second battalion artillery, four companies of the fourth battalion artillery—Lieutenant-colonel Trevelyan. Infantry: 20th regiment Native Infantry, 26th regiment Native Infantry—first brigade, Colonel Macan; 4th Bengal Native Infantry, 23rd regiment Native Light Infantry, Belooch battalion—second brigade, Colonel Honnor.

"5. The Lieutenant-general avails himself of this opportunity to return his warmest thanks to the whole of the troops placed under his command for service in Persia, for their very exemplary conduct since their arrival in this country, evinced by the fact of scarcely one instance of misconduct on the part of any individual having been brought to his notice. This entire absence of crime amongst so large a body of troops assembled in camp redounds to the credit of both officers and men, and is the strongest possible proof of the high state of discipline of the force; whilst their conduct throughout the expedition to Brásjoon, and in the engagement at Khoosh-aub, bore ample testimony to the gallantry of all ranks before an enemy, and to their cheerful and patient endurance of fatigue and hardship under most trying circumstances.

"6. Lieutenant-general Sir James Outram,

as a soldier who has been honoured with such a command, cannot help expressing his regret that more opportunity has not been afforded the troops by the enemy for the display of that prowess and gallant spirit which he knows to prevail amongst all ranks; but as a peace has been concluded by her gracious Majesty's government, it is a source of much satisfaction to the lieutenant-general that a great portion of the force is thus enabled to return at once to India before the monsoon commences; and he hopes that an early compliance on the part of the Persian government with the conditions of the treaty will shortly remove the necessity which still exists for a further occupation of Bushire.

"7. Whilst bidding farewell to the troops about to leave Persia, and wishing them a pleasant voyage and happy meeting with their families and friends in India, the lieutenant-general begs to assure that portion of the force to remain at Bushire that every care has been taken for their welfare, and that no exertion will be spared to render their short sojourn in this country as comfortable and as little injurious to their health as possible. Spacious barracks are in course of erection, and military materials of every description are being collected for their use.

"8. In conclusion, the lieutenant-general begs to offer his sincere thanks to all now about to return to India, especially to Brigadier-general Havelock, C.B., for the zealous and valuable assistance he has afforded him at all times, in command of the second division; and requests he will be so good as to convey to Brigadiers Hutt, Hale, and Hamilton, and to the general officers of his personal, divisional, and brigade staffs, as well as to the medical and departmental officers, a similar expression of his thanks for the valuable and efficient services they have performed.

"The Lieutenant-general has also to thank Brigadier Wilson, K.H., and his staff, who leave with the European infantry of the first division, and likewise Major Boye, deputy-judge-advocate-general, and the Rev. G. Watson, chaplain, who also returns to India.

"Signed by command,

"E. Lugard,

"Chief of the Staff."

On the 15th of May, Brigadier-general Havelock, with the staff of his late division, embarked on the steamer *Berenice*, which had so well carried him and the Highlanders past the batteries on the day of the capture. She sailed the following day for Bombay, having in tow the light battalion transport *Ocean Monarch*, which carried half of that regiment, the remainder being on the decks of the *Berenice*. On the afternoon previous to her departure the town of Mohammerah was given up to Sheik Jabber's tribe of Arabs, and the *Clive* sloop was left moored in the river, to prevent the Persians from molesting them, or entering the town before the evacuation of Herat should be certainly ascertained. The heat gradually increased, and became most oppressive during the passage down the Gulf, exciting feelings of commiseration for the division left encamped on the glaring sands of Bushire, and likely to occupy their warm quarters for some six months to come.

The land off Muscat was made on the 22nd of May, when, casting off the *Ocean Monarch* in the offing, the *Berenice* entered the picturesque, rock-bound harbour to coal. Its singular marine sentinel, if one may so term a huge grampus, or whale of the bottle-nose species, and named by the sailors "Muscat Tom," made his appearance, spouting at no great distance from the ship. This fish is said to have frequented the harbour for five or six years past, and to have cleared it effectually of sharks which before abounded—few days passing without this monster "guard-fish" appearing in one part or other of the harbour. This is of considerable size, a basin enclosed within a semicircle of precipitous, barren, abrupt rocks, without a particle of verdure or brush of the smallest kind, and so singularly resembling, both in colour and profile, the volcanic range round Aden, that it might be readily imagined to be a detached portion of the same. Three large castellated fortifications, each being distinct, with round towers of two stories, crown the abrupt cliffs immediately over the town, which stands on a natural terrace along the water's edge. Similar works, perched on almost inaccessible pinnacles, flank either side of the basin, with strong batteries at their bases, almost *à fleur d'eau*, the rocks on the left being isolated from the main land. A narrow outlet at the upper end on that side gives a most extraordinary effect to the glimpse of the coast landscape beyond seen through it, and which, in the morning sun-light, contrasted with the dark cliffs around, looked like a bright picture set in an ebony frame.

Were the fortifications in order the place would be impregnable from the sea—but all is falling into ruins; and the stronghold, built by the bold Genoese and Portuguese navigators long ago, will soon have scarce one stone left upon another. The guns mounted on the works are iron ships' ordnance of very ancient date, all honeycombed and rust destroyed. Some few pieces are kept in order, chiefly for firing salutes, every discharge of which shakes down masses of ruined masonry and rock, and lends a helping hand to the already too rapid destroyer, Time. A clumsy frigate, with one or two corvettes, were lying at anchor, with sails unbent, and apparently in ordinary. This naval force is kept up by the imaum for the protection of his trading craft from the Gulf pirates, who, though not so numerous as formerly, still abound, and occasionally commit acts of great daring and atrocity, not alone on his territory and shipping, but on both shores of the Gulf. They generally, however, carefully avoid any contact with the British flag—our exterminating policy with gentry of their profession, and the presence at all times of a very efficient little squadron to enforce respect in those waters, being perfectly well appreciated.

In addition to the more considerable works, nearly every crag around Muscat has its small tower; and formidable enough they may once have been, though at present simply picturesque—perched like eyries high in the air, and seeming almost ready to drop into their own shadows on the smooth surface of the bay beneath. Here a busy scene is indeed presented so soon as a strange ship makes her appearance—for one might almost imagine the entire population of Muscat to have at once taken the water. Fruit, fish, vegetables, wares of all kinds, and boat-loads of the Gulf sweetmeat called "hulwah," are at once alongside. The latter commodity is a strongly scented sickly tasting compound of almond paste, sugar, citron, and rose-water, boiled to a syrup, and then allowed to cool into a sticky consistency in round, shallow, clay dishes. Once seen in the act of preparation in the bazaar—a Nübian slave, elbow deep in a huge cauldron, mashing its contents through a set of ebony fingers which ever and anon find their way to his blubber mouth—and the beholder is pretty safe to reckon "hulwah" (the king of sweets—so say the Persians and Arabs)—among the abominations of the land. The canoes which bring off their yelling and screaming live freight deserve particular notice, being among the most graceful and carefully finished of the canoe description, and would be pretty objects on smooth waters at home. An enterprising skipper would find it to his advantage to try the speculation.

The imaum being absent at Zanzibar, where he retires during the hot months, no opportunity was afforded of seeing the grand sight of the place, viz., himself and his palace; and in attempting to make an inspection of one or two of the larger fortifications, some ruffianly looking Arabs in the lower batteries, by very significant signs, and handling of matchlocks and rusty sabres, prevented any ascent to examine the upper ones. The guns in one particular battery were tied to logs of timber instead of being mounted upon carriages, and woe betide the gunner who may ever attempt to discharge them—although from the water their muzzles grinning through their casemated portholes appeared warlike and threatening enough. The town and bazaars were filthy in the extreme, and the latter were thronged by so many dirty Hindostanees that they might have been mistaken for back streets in a low quarter of Bombay.

The sea face of Muscat, from the harbour, would make a beautiful drop-scene for a theatre—but, to preserve the illusion entire, travellers will do well not to raise the scene by a visit to the shore—for there every Eastern abomination, without one counter-balancing agreeable, will assuredly be met with. Leaving

Muscat on the 23rd of May, and picking up the *Ocean Monarch* outside the anchorage, the *Berenice* reached Bombay on the 29th, and had scarcely come to her moorings in the harbour when the astounding intelligence of the widely spread revolt in the Bengal native army, and of the atrocities committed by the sepoys, was received. With this came also the information that the Highlanders and 64th regiment had, without disembarking, been sent round to the scene of action—this portion of the old division in Persia thus finding a new though much to be lamented field for its services.

CHAPTER X.

Disasters at Sea—Conclusion.

FOLLOWING closely upon the track of these regiments of his old command, General Havelock and the officers belonging to them who had accompanied him in the *Berenice* again embarked, on the 1st of June, on the steamer *Erin*, of the Peninsular and Oriental Company, for Point de Galle, Ceylon—intending to continue the route to Calcutta by the *Bengal* steamer, expected from Suez, with the outcoming mail from England, about the period of the *Erin's* arrival at Galle.

The following were the party of the second division:—Brigadier-general Havelock, C.B.; Colonel Wilson, K.H., of 64th regiment, late commanding first brigade, first division; Captain Hunt, 78th Highlanders; Lieutenant Havelock, her Majesty's 10th regiment, deputy quarter-master-general, second division; and Lieutenant Johnson, 1st Oude Cavalry, attached to the Scinde Horse. There were several other passengers, naval officers and merchants, proceeding to the Straits and China, as well as to Ceylon. The early part of the voyage was made without accident; the extent of the Malabar coast, and all its rocky dangers, passed in safety. Cape Comorin was sighted, and the north end of Ceylon made during a beautiful afternoon on the 5th, when the ship's position was supposed to be accurately known; and arrival at Point de Galle predicted for early the ensuing day. The events, however, of a few short hours proved the utter folly and uselessness of human calculations or intentions.

During the evening the weather changed for the worse, the wind freshened, a bubble of a sea got up, and a misty haze prevented a clear look-out at any distance from the ship; towards midnight, also, heavy rain fell. None of these changes, however, excited the slightest uneasinesss, the bearings of the land being considered positive. When once the common precautions of taking in sail (a portion only), and providing against ordinary squally weather, had been made, the usual quiet and sense of security prevailed through the ship. The first notice of danger was given by the *Erin* striking heavily, about two o'clock in the morning, with a shock sufficient to throw every one off his legs, the hide tiller-ropes snapping immediately, and the ship consequently becoming unmanageable. A heavy squall, too, swept over us at the same time, and involved all in obscurity; although there was sufficient hazy light, assisted by vivid lightning, to make out breakers all around. On the rain ceasing, shortly after, the land was, to the surprise of all, perceived so close that the loom of the cocoa-nut trees seemed, through the mist, almost to overshadow the deck.

After the first shock the ship had glided into deep water again, and all were expecting her to go down by the head, as the fore part of the vessel had at once filled, when she struck again and again, and finally gave one long surge, which fixed two thirds of her length firmly upon the reef. This brought her up with a shock which made the whole frame shiver, and nearly jerked the masts out. The force of this may be imagined, as the speed at the time of its occurring was more than eleven knots the hour. The fate of the ship was now sealed, and the lives of those on board dependent, under Providence, on the time that wood and iron could hang together against the wind and sea then raging around.

To move about the decks became almost impossible, as every surge rolling in lifted the ship bodily, and receding, dashed her with violence against the bottom. It therefore became necessary to hang on to the sides or rigging for life; and heavy rain commencing again to fall, made the long hours until daylight wearisome and trying in the extreme. No persuasions could induce the Lascar crew to go aloft to remove the heavier sails or send the upper masts and yards down, and by lightening the top weight lessen the severity of the constant shocks. Huddled in groups wherever they could find shelter, they were almost useless throughout the night. Guns were fired and blue lights burned immediately it was ascertained that the accident was without remedy. These soon gave the alarm, and brought the district judge

(Mr. Templar, Ceylon Civil Service) and a crowd of fishermen and others to the beach to assist. One bold fellow swam off, though nearly drowned in the breakers, alongside the ship, and returning, when sufficiently recovered, with a line, a hawser was got on shore by which a communication was established.

So soon as it was sufficiently light, canoes came off, hauled along the hawser through the surf, and the passengers were all landed in two or three trips, without accident. About ten o'clock in the morning the mainmast fell, and very shortly afterwards the ship broke into three pieces,—the fore and after parts completely separating from the machinery in the centre, the weight of which kept it steady; the after-part of the vessel turning completely on its beam ends, with the deck half under water, facing the shore. Had this occurred before daybreak, with the sea then running, scarce a soul on board could have reached the shore alive. The treasure on board was saved, but not one iota of a costly cargo, valued at more than £200,000. Within little more than eight hours of her striking, a noble ship which seemed as perfect as human hands could make her, and strong enough almost to defy the power of wind or waves, rapidly broke up, and the sea and beach around were covered with the *débris* of her wreck. Valuable furniture, pictures, pier glasses, stores, dressing-cases, nautical instrument cases, hat-boxes, and air-tight trunks, floated about in admirable confusion among oars, hencoops, broken boats, spars, gratings, and other loose fittings of the decks. Sheep might be seen swimming for their lives, but perversely heading out to sea, with cocks and hens very much out of their element, and geese who seemed rather to enjoy the matter than otherwise.

The accident happened off Caltura, a small civil station about half way between Galle and Colombo; and fortunate was it for us all that the *Erin* struck where she did, as only one mile above the spot and three below it, rocky reefs project into the sea with deep water around. Had she touched upon one of these, she must have gone down without leaving a trace of our fate. Through the kindness of the judge (to whose hospitality we were greatly indebted) conveyances were procured to take us on to Galle, where, arriving early on the 7th of June, the Government steamer *Fire Queen* was fortunately found lying at anchor, as our accident had made us too late to proceed to Calcutta by the Bengal steamer from Suez. Great excitement prevailed in Ceylon regarding news from India, and the island was almost denuded of European troops. Her Majesty's 37th regiment and a company of Royal Artillery had been sent to Calcutta but a few days previous to our arrival.

General Havelock and the remainder of our Persian party again embarked on the 8th of June; and the *Fire Queen* went to sea immediately afterwards. On the 12th she entered the Madras roadstead, when great surprise and some alarm of a disaster was created by observing the colours on the fort flagstaff and all the shipping to be hoisted half mast high.

This was shortly afterwards explained by intelligence of the melancholy death of the Commander-in-chief in India, Lieutenant-general Sir George Anson. He died very suddenly, of cholera, while actually marching to re-capture Delhi from the mutineers, who some short time previously had seized it under circumstances of great atrocity. Information from up country, now daily received, but too fully confirmed the fact that not simple local disaffection, but a blow at the very existence of British power in India had been aimed by the treacherous army. The outbreak must have been for many months contemplated, and the issue of some newly constructed cartridges—which they complained of as being intended to destroy religious caste among them by defiling them with grease of either bullocks or pigs—simply put forward as a blind.

Government, however, seemed aroused to the necessity of adopting most vigorous measures; and the services of the *Fire Queen* were at once secured to convey to Calcutta the Commander-in-chief of Madras, Lieutenant-general Sir Patrick Grant, to whom the chief command of the Bengal presidency was committed by the Governor-general. This was a post for which long and gallant services with the army in rebellion, as their adjutant-general, peculiarly fitted Sir Patrick Grant.

With this distinguished addition to her passengers, the *Fire Queen* left immediately for Bengal, and arrived without accident at Calcutta on the 17th of June. The arrival of two men so fitted for a great crisis as the new military commander and the veteran chief of the Persian second division, was gladly welcomed; and fresh vigour seemed to be infused into the preparations then in progress.

Here a new field for adventure, though a melancholy one for military distinction, opened out to the comrade regiments in Persia. The author therefore closes these rough sketches of scenes which enlivened camp life and left many pleasing reminiscences of friends and adventures with the second division in Persia.

www.ingramcontent.com/pod-product-compliance
Ingram Content Group UK Ltd.
Pitfield, Milton Keynes, MK11 3LW, UK
UKHW041952190726
13854UKWH00005B/1927

9 781845 742065